ANTHROPOLOGICAL PAPERS OF
THE UNIVERSITY OF ARIZONA
NUMBER 22

SOCIAL FUNCTIONS OF LANGUAGE IN A MEXICAN-AMERICAN COMMUNITY

GEORGE C. *carpenter* BARKER, 1912-1958,
||

THE UNIVERSITY OF ARIZONA PRESS
TUCSON, ARIZONA 1972

About the Author ...

GEORGE CARPENTER BARKER (1912–1958) combined his wide-ranging interests with a well-balanced professional background. He received both the M.A. and Ph.D. degrees in anthropology from the University of Chicago, the latter in 1947. Previously he had received an undergraduate degree in history from the University of California, Los Angeles, and an M.S. degree in journalism from Columbia University.

His first major research project was field work in Tucson, resulting in the dissertation from which this present monograph has been adapted. While a Research Associate in the Department of Anthropology, University of Arizona, 1947–48, Barker did additional field work concerning the social functions of language in a cross-cultural situation, with special reference to Mexican-American youths.

From 1950 until his death he was a Research Associate in the Department of Anthropology and Sociology at UCLA, carrying on several research projects involving field work. He concentrated on studying Mexican-American youths in the Los Angeles area, but also continued his interests in folklore and the religious ceremonies of various Southwest Indian tribes, especially the Yaqui.

Despite increasing physical disability, Barker continued his travels, research, and writing until the day of his death. He was the author of a number of articles in scholarly journals, and of *Pachuco*.

A member of a large number of professional societies in several fields, Barker was also elected a Fellow of the American Anthropological Association and a Corresponding Member of the Asociación Española de Etnología y Folklore, Madrid.

Second printing 197.
First printing 197.

THE UNIVERSITY OF ARIZONA PRESS

I.S.B.N.-0-8165-0317-(
L.C. No. 70-18623?

FOREWORD

GEORGE CARPENTER BARKER was both a cultural anthropologist and an anthropological linguist. As a cultural anthropologist he was deeply interested in knowing how groups of people functioned as societies and developed distinct cultures. As an anthropological linguist he sought to understand the relationship between language and the total culture pattern.

Culture patterns are constantly changing. These changes may be, and usually are, accelerated in situations of contact with one or more other cultures. A question that interests both cultural anthropologists and linguists is whether or not the language usages of any particular society change concurrently with other aspects of that society's culture. Are changes in language usage uniform in a society undergoing general cultural change, or are there variations? If there are variations in language usage in a group undergoing change, can these variations be correlated with developing differences in the society and its culture generally? As the functions of the various aspects of a culture change, do the functions of the language change correspondingly? Barker states his central problem to be: "What degree of congruence, if any, may exist between the language usage of individuals in process of cultural change, and the social context of assimilation and acculturation in which this linguistic behavior occurs?"

With these questions concerning cultural change in mind, coupled with his ability to speak and understand Spanish, George Barker selected Tucson, Arizona, as the locale for his field studies.

In the mid-1940s, when Barker did his research, Tucson had a rather large group of people of Mexican ancestry. These people had attained various degrees of assimilation and acculturation. This community provided an ideal setting for research on the extent and degree of correlation between sociocultural change generally and variations in language usage. Barker had the ability to learn and use (a) what he calls "standard Mexican Spanish," (b) the Sonoran dialect, and (c) the southern Arizona dialect. He established his residence in a Mexican barrio where he was in daily contact with Spanish-speaking people in a great variety of contexts. In addition, he maintained numerous contacts with people of Mexican ancestry in other barrios and throughout the community of Tucson. His field experience brought him into constant contact with individuals, families, and organizations representing a wide range of cultural change and variation in language usage.

The results of Barker's research and analysis, which are presented in this publication, constituted his doctoral dissertation at the University of Chicago in 1947.

The study of linguistics has become much more complex in the intervening years. New theories have been developed. The linguistic theoretician will find here only the most elementary ideas of present-day ethnolinguistics. However, these ideas were developing at the time this study was made.

This monograph is valuable because it does present ideas that were new in the mid-1940s. Furthermore, these ideas were tested in a field study involving language usages current at that time. As a result we have data concerning language usage in a context of culture change, the extent to which there was variation in such usage, and an indication of the extent to which such variations in language usage could be correlated with change in other aspects of culture. The student interested in linguistic and other cultural change generally has here a baseline for further studies in linguistic and general cultural change. The ethnic group studied by Barker — the people of Mexican ancestry — form an important segment of Tucson's population in the 1970s, as they did when the study was made.

In this monograph Barker uses the two terms, Mexican-American and Mexican, interchangeably when referring to the people of Mexican ancestry. The term Mexican is used to a greater extent than Mexican-American as a matter of convenience in writing, in the same way that he uses the terms Anglo and Chinese to refer to Anglo-Americans and Chinese-Americans.

HARRY T. GETTY
The University of Arizona

ACKNOWLEDGMENTS

Grateful acknowledgment is made to the Department of Anthropology, University of Chicago, for a grant in linguistic research for the field work of this study. The writer also wishes to express his appreciation to Dr. A. M. Halpern for many suggestions in the planning and conduct of this research, to Professor Harry T. Getty of the University of Arizona for invaluable assistance in the field, and to Professors W. Lloyd Warner, Norman McQuown, and Robert Redfield of the University of Chicago for critical advice and suggestions in the later stages of the inquiry.

The writer also owes much to Dr. Harry Hoijer of the Department of Anthropology, University of California at Los Angeles, for reading and commenting upon various sections of the manuscript. Others whose generous assistance should be mentioned include Dr. Fay-Cooper Cole of the University of Chicago; Dr. E. H. Spicer of the University of Arizona; Miss Gertrude Hill, librarian in the same university; Mrs. George F. Kitt of the Arizona Pioneers' Historical Society; Dr. Kurt H. Wolff of Ohio State University; Mrs. María López de Lowther and Miss Charleen Daggs of the Spanish department, and Margaret Case and Dr. Harry W. Case of the departments of Psychology and Engineering, UCLA.

Finally, the writer wishes to express his deep indebtedness to his informants and to his father and mother, George and Olive Barker, for help and encouragement throughout the project.

GEORGE C. BARKER
1947

CONTENTS

Chapter 1

THE SOCIAL FUNCTIONS OF LANGUAGE

This thesis is an inquiry into how language functions in the life of a bilingual minority group in process of cultural change. Since the subjects of this study are individuals of Mexican descent living in the American community of Tucson, Arizona, 60 miles from the Mexican border, the type of cultural change involved is both one of acculturation, involving the continuous firsthand contact of representatives of two different cultures, and of assimilation, involving the gradual engulfing of representatives of one culture, and their absorption into the dominant group.

The central problem of this thesis may be stated as "How, if at all, may the linguistic behavior of members of the bilingual minority group be related to other aspects of their social behavior?" This question was provoked by the observation that bilinguals having the same general background and living in the same general community, often display wide variations in their linguistic behavior, both in respect to their usage of the ancestral language and in their usage of English. Are these variations the results of unrecognized uniformities in the way language functions in the lives of these people, or must such variations be attributed to chance? How does it happen, for example, that among bilinguals, the ancestral language will be used on one occasion and English on another, and that on certain occasions bilinguals will alternate, without apparent cause, from one language to another? Again, how is it that certain bilinguals will deliberately avoid speaking the ancestral language with outsiders, even though they know that the outsider understands and speaks their language, while other bilinguals will go out of their way to get outsiders to speak the language, and will take great pleasure in helping them learn its subtleties?

As an approach to this problem, we may first attempt to survey briefly what is known about the social functions of language in the life of monolingual social groups. By social functions of language is meant the ways in which the language spoken by a group of people is related to that group's social position and organization. To clarify this sociological view of language, we should distinguish it at the outset of this study from the older psychological approach which sought to determine the relation between language and thought. According to this older view, the main function of language was to express or communicate "mental content." The assumptions involved in this earlier view were that language was simply a vehicle for the expression and transmission of "ideas" and that its function was merely technical in the "mental life" and "material culture" of the group. Until the beginning of the present century this view was widely held by social theorists, who took correspondingly little interest in language as a source of data on social organization.

The beginning of interest in the social functions of language may be traced to several sources. One, of course, was the science of linguistics, whose pioneer workers were impressed by the relation of speech forms to class status and prestige. Another was the early field work of Lewis H. Morgan and others in anthropology, which indicated significant relationships between kinship nomenclature and social usages. Another source was the group of French sociologists headed by Emile Durkheim, whose theory of collective representations aroused interest in the categories of a language as determinants in social behavior (Dorozewski 1933). Still later, research in the sociology of knowledge has shown interesting relationships between word-meanings and the various social groups using these words (Mannheim 1936; Armbruster 1944).

Interest in language as sociological data also arose through the behaviorist school of psychology. Basing their theories on the observation of animal and human actions, the early behaviorists claimed that "thought" was merely subvocal speech. This view, so diametrically opposed to that of mentalistic psychology, led to renewed interest on the part of social psychologists in the study of language behavior. Gradually, through observational studies of animal groups, children's groups, and preliterate or "primitive" societies, a new attitude toward language began to develop. One of the landmarks of this development was the work of de Laguna (1927), who held that a basic function of human speech was to coordinate the activity of the group. Malinowski (1923, 1935) took a similar view in his analysis of the language behavior of the Trobriand Islanders: to the Trobriand native, language is a definite part of ritual activity, and often is the equivalent of action. Finally, the study of children's groups led Piaget (1926), Mead (1934), and others to focus attention on the child's use of language as a process of socialization, whereby he achieves reflective thinking through taking the role of others in his speech behavior (Lorimer 1929).

To Mead, Dewey (1925), and other social behaviorists, language was an integral part of the total behavior of the organism. The implications of this view to social science were profound, since it meant that much which had previously been relegated to the introspective psychologist as "mental life" was now open to observation and analysis. The older behaviorism had been limited to descriptions of overt behavior below the verbal level. Now, with the new approach to speech, the entire field of symbolic behavior was made available for systematic investigation. Whereas the older behaviorism had tended to describe human behavior as an aspect of animal behavior, the new viewpoint brought out striking differences. These differences, as indicated by Mead, Korzybski, White (1944), and others, hinged on the function of the symbol or sign in human and animal life. While many animal groups coordinate their activities by means of vocal signs, such cries have no significance apart from the context of the immediate situation. Human beings, on the contrary, are conscious of the function of signs as symbols, and need not react automatically to them. In Mead's (1934) terminology, animals can react to symbols but not to significant symbols. In Korzybski's (1933) terminology, animals have signal reactions, but only humans have symbol (fully flexible) reactions. Many writers have emphasized the importance of this point in the understanding of human culture. By the same token, an understanding of the role of the symbol is critical to any study of the social functions of language.

The term "symbol" is used in this thesis in the sense of an arbitrary sign, established by social or personal usage, which has acquired meaning for the group or individual. It is thus to be distinguished from the nonsymbolic "sign" made by an animal. A sign cannot be understood apart from its accompanying situation. A symbol can be understood in any situation, provided its usage in a universe of discourse is known. By "universe of discourse" is meant not merely the verbal context of a symbol but the whole system of assumptions and connotations associated with the language of individuals within a given social group (Mannheim 1936).

Besides its various social meanings a symbol may have distinct personal meanings or values, dependent upon the way in which that particular symbol has been associated within the experience of any given individual. The words "strawberry jam," for example, may have a favorable, or positive, symbolic value to many English-speaking persons, but to one who has recently suffered an attack of food poisoning after eating this type of preserves, it is likely to have a negative symbolic connotation. This tendency of people to develop personal symbolic values through experience seems to hold true not only of words, but of many other aspects of the social environment, from neighborhoods and articles of dress to languages and dialects. In short, this means that to humans the "objects" of the environment function as symbols with multiple values — a situation which does not seem to obtain among animals.

While the coordination of group activity now is widely accepted as a basic social function of language, little attempt has been made to establish a systematic classification covering the whole field of such social functions. Perhaps the closest approach to such a classification was made by Sapir (1921: 159–60), who suggested that in addition to the general functions of language in the spheres of thought, communication, and expression, there are a number of "special derivations" which may be considered social functions of language:

1. Language as a form of socialization. This would include the service of communication between members of a group, the service of a common dialect or subform of language as a symbol of social solidarity, and the service of establishing rapport between members of a physical group.

2. Language as a culture-preserving instrument, whereby cultural forms are transmitted from generation to generation.

3. Language as a factor in the growth of individuality, or development of social personality.

4. Language as a declaration of the psychological place held by the various members of the group.

Sapir emphasized the importance of what he called the "expressive" aspect of language in the social life of the group. His third category, above, refers to the way in which an individual's language habits, or manner of speaking, helps to identify him as a distinct personality in the group, while the fourth category refers to the way in which the individual's manner of speaking reflects an attitude of dominance, equality, or subordination with respect to other members of the group.

Another pioneer effort to classify the social functions of language was made by McGranahan (1936: 206). Reviewing the "social uses" of language, he outlined three: (1) the coordination of activity, (2) the transmission of culture, and (3) the determination of national individuality. All three are included in Sapir's first two categories, above, and so need not be discussed here. McGranahan concluded his survey with a list of what he called "social misuses" of language: (1) word magic, the false identification of words with objects; (2) illogical persuasion, the use of sacred or emotionally charged words in place of logic in argument; (3) the substance fallacy — the notion that where there is a word, there must be an actual substance or condition that corresponds to that word; and (4) verbal nonsense, the use of terms in such a way that they function merely as "meaningless noises." These and other social misuses of language are treated more elaborately in a number of works dealing with semantics, notably the volumes by Korzybski (1933), Chase (1939), Hayakawa (1941), and Lee (1941). It is not within the scope of this study to enter into a discussion of these misuses, except to point out their general relationship to the present field of inquiry. Morris (1938: 10) has outlined this relationship in a discussion of semiosis, the "science of signs." He divides this science into three sections: syntactics, the study of language structure; semantics, the empirical study of the relation of signs to objects; and pragmatics, the investigation of language as a type of communicative activity, social in origin and nature. By "semantics" Morris refers to the traditional use of the the term (Malinowski 1923), which should be distinguished from the theory of "general semantics" formulated by Korzybski. While it probably

is true that any study of language touches in some degree all three of Morris' subdivisions, the present study of the social functions of language may be characterized as centering in the field of pragmatics.

In addition to the classifications of Sapir and McGranahan, mentioned above, many pertinent observations and suggestions as to the social functions of language have been made by different scientists in a more informal way, and it may be well to review some of these suggestions.

Malinowski (1923) recognized a functional difference between language as a part of action and language as "phatic communion," engaged in simply as a social amenity. The term "phatic communion" is approximately equivalent to Sapir's (1921) "establishment of rapport," and also is paralleled by Dewey's (1925) term "consummatory," or language spoken as an end in itself. Like Malinowski, Dewey uses this term in opposition to the active, referential function of language, which he calls "instrumental." Hayakawa (1941) recognizes a similar distinction with his "presymbolic" and "symbolic" types of language.

The function of language in indicating status relationships has been noted by many students of linguistics. Bloomfield (1933) points out that what is called "good" and "bad" grammar may be more accurately described as "standard" and "substandard," the former being the particular form enjoying social prestige. Schlauch (1942) has an interesting discussion of class dialects in relation to common and polite speech forms. A work by Vendryes (1925: 249–59) draws attention to what he calls "special languages" — languages employed only by groups of individuals placed in special circumstances. Examples are the language of the law, ecclesiastical language, criminal argots, and all forms of slang. Such languages, according to Vendryes, are the result of social divisions and draw sustenance from the common language of the larger social group.

The above attempts to describe and classify the social functions of language may be regrouped under three main social functions. The first of these is the function of language in defining the group as a group. For convenience, we may call this the group-defining function. Sapir's description of language as a socializing force and as a culture-preserving instrument comes under this heading as do all three of McGranahan's social uses. The common language coordinates the activities of the group, makes individuals conscious of their membership, sets up an in-group-out-group relationship between members and strangers, and enables the group to retain its distinctive characteristics over many generations.

The second main social function of language is to define social relations within the group. This may be referred to as the group-relating function. Under this heading come Sapir's last two points — language as a factor in social personality and as a declaration of the individual's psychological place in the group — as well as Schlauch's class dialects and Vendryes' special languages. Thus language may reflect both the social structure of a society and the relation of the individual to that structure.

A third main social function of language, not adequately described in either of the above categories, is that of defining the character of the interpersonal relations between individuals. Sapir has suggested this function in his description of language as a declaration of "psychological place." But it is not only position but the character of personal relations which is involved. Further, we are concerned here not only with the relation of group members to each other, but with their relations with outsiders as well. Forms of address, for example, not only define the position of the individual in the group; they also define the relations between individuals, who may belong to quite different groups. Moreover, they serve to indicate whether these relations are to be conducted on a plane of formality, informality, or intimacy. Many languages have special declensions for the expression of intimate relations. English lacks these declensions but has compensated for it through the use, in intimate relations, of such forms as "dear," "darling," "honey," and the like.

Having briefly reviewed the functions of language in the life of the social group, let us now turn to a more detailed consideration of how language functions under conditions of culture contact. In the first place, we may note that in most instances of contact between social groups having different cultures, we are dealing not with one but with two or more languages. There are the languages of the two groups, and possibly even a third language developed through combination of the other two,

as, for instance, the development of pidgin English in the South Pacific. The problem of how languages change under conditions of culture contact already has received careful attention on the part of anthropologists and linguists. Also, some valuable work has been done on the problem of the relation between linguistic change and other aspects of the acculturation process. The work of Spicer (1943) has indicated that the introduction of loan-words from Spanish and English into the Yaqui vocabulary may be correlated, to some degree, with different historic periods in Yaqui acculturation. A parallel study, made by Johnson (1943), has indicated that while the Spanish language has influenced every aspect of the Yaqui language and social life, it has not destroyed or altered the fundamental integrity of Yaqui culture.

Anthropologists and sociologists engaged in field studies of the life of a group in process of culture contact have frequently noted that, where two languages are involved, the functions formerly performed by one language come to be divided between two or more. This division seems to be based part on convenience and part on necessity. Individuals brought up in the language of their ancestral culture seem to find it easier to talk to each other in that language, and to outsiders in the language of the outsider's culture. Some investigators have suggested that a logical outcome of this division is that the ethnic language comes to symbolize the group and its cultural background — for individuals both inside and outside the ethnic group — or, as we have already indicated, to identify the group as a group. This point has been advanced by many students of acculturation and assimilation. Redfield (1930), in his study of Tepotztlán, showed how the native Indian language, rather than Spanish, became a symbol of local patriotism. Similarly, Reuter (1946), discussing culture contacts in Puerto Rico, has shown how the impact of western culture has outmoded Spanish, the folk language of Puerto Rico, and at the same time has changed it from a tool to a sacred value.

A second and equally important inference regarding this division in linguistic function is that the individual's skill in using the language of a second or adopted culture comes to symbolize his status in the new society. For the uneducated immigrant this situation seems to impose a heavy penalty. Tuck

(1946), in her study of a Mexican-American community in California, suggests that the failure of Mexican laborers to use their faulty English in public constitutes the principal reason for the feeling on the part of many Anglo-Americans that the Mexican cannot be assimilated — or in short, that he should have no status at all in the community. Bossard (1945) has summarized this relation of language to status of bilingual groups by pointing out that in the United States and in all countries where there are linguistic minorities, the process of linguistic identification with status operates in two dimensions rather than in one. Here, he points out, in addition to the determination of status based on conformity to one socially accepted form of expression, there is the added dimension of bilingualism, for many persons, operating against a historical background of immigrant sequence and minority-group status. In this added dimension, he suggests, a second language and its vestiges are bound up with the status of the particular minority group that speaks that language.

Bossard's study is concerned primarily with the effect on personality of development in a bilingual family. Using material from seventeen case studies, he shows how the bilingual situation affects child development through the child's problem of learning two languages, expressing himself in both, and overcoming the ridicule of playmates. He further shows how, to shield himself against the consequences of bilinguality, the child develops a number of protective devices, such as a restrained manner of speaking, inconspicuous behavior, home avoidance, and strenuous efforts to speak perfect English even at the expense of sacrificing friendship. He then goes on to show how the vestiges of a bilingual background limit the occupational opportunities of the adult. In short, while Bossard's work touches only incidentally on the "process" aspect of culture contact, it does clearly suggest the ways in which bilingualism may act as a determinant in this process.

In his discussion of the linguistic behavior of bilinguals, Bossard confines himself almost entirely to two aspects: first, the individual's proficiency in English and, second, his use or avoidance of the ethnic language. This leaves undescribed several other important aspects of the linguistic behavior of bilinguals, especially of individuals in process of cultural change. One of these aspects is the individual's proficiency in the ethnic language. Does he speak a standard form of the language? Does he speak a local dialect? Or does he speak a hybrid language composed of both his ancestral and adopted tongues? Another important aspect relates to his usage of the alternative linguistic means at his command. When conversing with other bilinguals, under what conditions does he use the ancestral language, or the adopted language, or a form borrowed from either?

In the literature of acculturation and assimilation there are many other works which contain some reference to the language used by the people studied. Some of these bear close relation to our problem. As part of a study of the psychological aspects of acculturation, Child (1943) made an investigation of the language habits of Italian-Americans in New Haven, Connecticut. Using case studies of more than fifty Italian-American boys, he found that his subjects could be grouped into three types of reaction — the in-group, the rebel, and the apathetic — according to their acceptance, rejection, or apathy toward the Italian group in the community. For each of these groups, he reported on the language habits, or, more specifically, the relative use of Italian dialect, standard Italian, and English. His findings indicated that individuals having the in-group reaction spoke the most Italian dialect, those having apathetic reactions spoke the least Italian, and those with the rebel reaction had a great variation in their habits, perhaps resulting in part from their perception that knowledge of standard Italian may have prestige value in some parts of the American community. Child did not attempt to investigate in detail the type of situation in which his informants had their choice of alternate languages.

Changes in language habits in relation to changes in family structure are cited by Humphrey (1944). He reports that in Detroit, among families of first-generation immigrants, the traditional four-level family hierarchy of Mexico (father, mother, sons, daughters) changes to one of roughly two levels, with the position of the sons almost on a level with that of the father, and that of the daughters approximately that of the mother. In this new alignment, he reports, it is customary for the children to speak English among themselves and Spanish to their parents. After the children marry, he notes, there are further changes in both family structure and language habits. The wife's subordination is now almost nominal, and the young couple drops their Spanish altogether.

The possible relation between language content or terminology, and the type of racial attitudes and relations in an acculturation situation was investigated by Rogler (1944). He found that the terms used by Puerto Ricans to describe various situations involving racial relations did not necessarily reflect the attitudes of the people using the terms, and that, furthermore, the terms used did not cover the range of interracial situations involved. He concluded that while semantics may be useful as one type of approach to the study of racial distance, it is not reliable as an index to basic relationships.

The above-mentioned investigations, of course, do not exhaust the field, but do illustrate the type of work that has been done to date in the area of our problem. All represent attempts to see how some one aspect of linguistic behavior may be related to the social participation of the members of a minority group in process of cultural change. Considered from a broader viewpoint, language habits, terminology, foreign accent, command of English, usage in the family, and the like, are parts of what may be described as the linguistic system of the particular individual or group involved. The present thesis will depart from the above studies, therefore, by considering not one aspect of linguistic structure, but the total linguistic behavior pattern of individuals and groups in relation to their social participation.

This brings us to the two basic postulates of the present investigation. The first of these is that the linguistic behavior of any given individual exhibits a systematic patterning that can be defined objectively in terms, first, of the limits of the system, second, of the parts of which it is composed, and, third, of the relative frequency of use of the various parts in standard situations. In studying the linguistic behavior of a bilingual in process of cultural change, then, we are interested in seeing precisely what languages and dialects he speaks, what grammatical expressions and phrases he uses in various situations, and with what frequency he selects one language, dialect, or expression in preference to an alternative. We may describe this investigation of patterns of linguistic behavior as the study of language usage.

The second basic postulate of this study is that language, through its function of entering intimately into the definition and constant redefinition of all interpersonal relations, indicates the limits and the categories of the interpersonal relations into which a given individual enters. (By "interpersonal relations" is meant the nature of the social relations — whether formal, informal, supraordinated, subordinated, personal, or impersonal — in effect between two or more individuals.) Assuming that the type of language usage manifested in a given social context is congruent with the nature of the social context itself, we thus have the possibility of describing the total social relations of a given individual with something approaching the systematic clarity with which we can define the same individual's linguistic behavior.

Returning to the central problem of our investigation, we may say at once that the weakest link in the above argument is our assumption that language usage is congruent with other aspects of social behavior. Our investigation, therefore, will be designed to see what degree of congruence, if any, may exist between the language usage of individuals in process of cultural change, and the social context of assimilation and acculturation in which this linguistic behavior occurs.

Chapter 2

STATEMENT OF THE PROBLEM

We have defined the problem of this thesis as an inquiry into how language functions in the life of a bilingual minority in process of cultural change, with the aim of seeing whether such functions can account for the wide variation in linguistic behavior among bilinguals having the same general cultural background and living in the same general community. As an approach to this problem, a series of hypotheses have, at various stages in the inquiry, been set up and tested. Thus, variations in linguistic behavior:

1. May be accounted for on the basis that the functions of language differ according to the socio-economic class of which the bilingual individual is a member.

2. May be accounted for in terms of the stage in the assimilation process which the individual has reached.

3. May be accounted for in terms of the social participation of the ethnic family in the social system.

4. May be accounted for in terms of the different symbolic values which, by reason of his social experience, the individual ascribes to the ethnic language and to English.

5. Must be ascribed largely to chance.

To prove or disprove any or all of the above hypotheses, detailed evidence of two general types is needed — one sociological and the other linguistic:

1. Sociological data on:
   a) the social structure of the general community in which the bilingual group is located;
   b) the social structure of the bilingual ethnic community and its relative position in the social system of the general community;
   c) the distribution and social participation of bilinguals in, first, the ethnic group and, second, the general social system of the community;
   d) the cultural background and family structure of families representing different ethnic generations and different socioeconomic statuses.

2. Linguistic data on:
   a) the character of the languages and dialects used by members of the bilingual group and by members of the majority group in the community;
   b) the way in which representative bilinguals use and react to these various languages and dialects.

With this outline in mind, let us now attempt to see what aspects of the evidence may be considered critical in proving or disproving each of the above hypotheses.

For hypothesis 1 to be proved, we would expect to find that bilingual individuals in different socioeconomic classes manifested correspondingly different patterns of linguistic behavior, and that there would be no difference in linguistic behavior between individuals in the same socioeconomic class.

For hypothesis 2 to be proved, we would expect to find that individuals in different stages of the assimilation process would manifest correspondingly different patterns of linguistic behavior, and that no two individuals in the same stage of this process would manifest different types of linguistic behavior.

For hypothesis 3 to be proved, we would expect that the linguistic behavior of the various members of any given bilingual family would follow the same general pattern, and that families whose social participation differed from others would have clearly defined differences in their patterns of linguistic behavior.

For hypothesis 4 to be proved, we would expect to find that individuals having the same relation to other ethnic individuals, to the ethnic community, and to non-ethnics, would have the same patterns of linguistic behavior. Correspondingly, individuals whose relations to other ethnics, to the ethnic community, and to non-ethnics differed from each other, would be expected to have distinctly different patterns of linguistic behavior.

For hypothesis 5 to be proved, we would expect that the linguistic variations would be so complex and have so little uniformity that no other hypothesis could be entertained.

Procedure

In the writer's M.A. thesis (1943), a tentative classification of the social functions of language was set up, and thirteen case studies were presented as examples of the language usage by ethnic individuals in a variety of social contexts. The results of the study indicated a definite relationship between the type of language usage, the type of social background, and the type of psychological adjustment to the assimilation situation in each case. These correlations suggested that the further development of this line of research would constitute a fruitful new approach to assimilation problems, and might be expected to yield data on certain factors of assimilation not fully revealed through the study of material culture and social organization alone. Specifically, such an investigation might help to answer such questions as:

1. Is there a general pattern of change in language usage which may be correlated with various stages in the assimilation process?
2. To what extent may changes in language use be correlated with (a) changes in family structure, and (b) differences in personality?
3. How is the individual's language use related to his social mobility and status in (a) the ethnic community, and (b) the larger non-ethnic community?

The method of inquiry which seemed best fitted for this type of research problem was that of the case study. Out of a single ethnic community it was proposed to select a number of individuals as representing (1) a cross section of the community's social system, and (2) a proportionate sampling of the community in terms of length of residence. Through informal observation and contacts over a period of at least six months it was proposed to examine the language usage of these individuals from the standpoint of both in-group and out-group relations. The comparative study of these cases, in various stages of the assimilation process, it was felt, might also make possible the compilation of a "natural history" of language usage in the community.

To obtain the type of data needed for this study, it was recognized that each individual's use of language (including both the ancestral language or dialect and English) would have to be studied in relation to his various roles in the social system. This was seen to involve (1) the making of an itemized list of the individual's social relations, (2) noting the language or dialect used with greatest frequency in each relation, and (3) noting how the language use between any two individuals may change in different social situations, as, for example:

(a) Situations in which the two are alone, or think they are;
(b) Situations in which only the immediate family is present;
(c) Situations in which only the extended family is present;
(d) Situations in which only other ethnic individuals are present;
(e) Situations in which non-ethnic individuals are present; and
(f) Situations involving emotional crisis.

It was felt that the type of ethnic community chosen for this study should be preferably a fairly compact, definitely set-off group within an urban area. The ethnic language preferably would be Spanish, since the writer understood and spoke it. The group would include a stable element of older immigrants and their children as well as an element representative of more recent migratory movements, thus making possible the comparative study of these three segments (parental generation, younger native-born generation, and recent immigrants) with their correspondingly different social backgrounds.

The technique of obtaining the material would be through casual conversations and observations designed to bring out the reactions of the individual to his ancestral language and English in a variety of situations. Not only family pressures but pressures from outside the group would be evaluated in their relationship to language usage. Direct questions of the order of, "Do you enjoy speaking English?" would be avoided. The aim would be rather to use indirect questions such as, "How did you get along at school?" to reveal the individual's frank assessment of his own language usage. Special effort would be made to bring out anecdotal material — episodes in the subject's life which might illustrate his language and other social behavior in specific assimilation situations.

The above suggested procedure was outlined by the writer following conferences with his adviser, A. M. Halpern of the department of anthropology, University of Chicago, in 1943. In 1945, after a series of survey trips to various California and Arizona towns having Mexican minorities, the city of Tucson was chosen as a testing ground for the hypotheses of this thesis largely for two reasons: first, the range of social positions occupied by the town's Mexican-American population was unusually wide, thereby permitting a comparative analysis of linguistic and other social behavior of individuals in different social settings and, second, an investigation of ethnic relations in Tucson, already being conducted by Harry Getty of the Department of Anthropology, University of Arizona, had made available to the writer much basic data on Tucson's social structure. This material, collected by Getty over a period of three years, provided the foundation for the present inquiry.

In the course of this inquiry, the field work for which extended over a six-month period in Tucson, the writer collected material on the language usage and social life of representative individuals and families of Mexican descent. In the final stages of the inquiry, a review of the data led to the tentative hypotheses outlined in this chapter. The first three of those hypotheses had to be eliminated from the present inquiry when it was discovered that individuals in the same socioeconomic class, the same stage in the assimilation process, and even within the same family, displayed wide variations in language usage. This discovery, however, should not be interpreted as invalidating the above propositions. Such wide variations in personal usage are only indicative of the fact that the analysis of the specific situation, when it goes beyond the rough language or dialect level, can be extremely complex. This in turn indicates that for a real test of the first three propositions, one must have as a basis, not only the choice of particular languages or dialects in particular cultural situations, but also the choice of specific forms in these languages or dialects in such situations. This problem will be discussed further in Chapter 4.

Since the first three propositions were eliminated from this inquiry, and since hypothesis 5 simply attributes to chance such variations in linguistic behavior, hypothesis 4 is the one with which we will be chiefly concerned in the balance of this thesis. This hypothesis, together with its several corollaries, is restated below.

In a bilingual minority group in process of cultural change, the functions originally performed by the ancestral language are divided between two or more languages, with the result that each language comes to be identified with certain specific fields of interpersonal relations. Thus for each individual, language takes on symbolic values which vary according to the individual's social experience. The character of this experience, in turn, depends on, first, the position of the minority group in the general community; second, the relation of the individual to the bilingual group; and, third, the relation of the individual to the general community. Certain corollaries follow:

1. The individual's pattern of linguistic behavior is congruent with his system of interpersonal relations.
2. The group's pattern of linguistic behavior is congruent with its system of interpersonal relations.
3. The linguistic behavior patterns of the bilingual individual and group may be used as indices of the conditions of assimilation and acculturation in the area studied.

Methods and Techniques of Study

The study of the social behavior of bilinguals involves both a sociological and linguistic analysis of the bilingual community. It has already been indicated that much of the needed sociological data was made available to the writer through previous research. In analyzing this material the writer followed the general procedure outlined by Warner and Lunt (1941). The linguistic analysis had three aspects: first, the collection of linguistic forms encountered in the community; second, the description and classification of these forms; and, third, the observation and recording of how different bilingual individuals in the community used and reacted to these alternative forms in varying situations, or, in short, the study of the language usage.

The study of the linguistic forms of a community involves the classification of its languages and dialects and their descriptive analysis in terms of linguistic structure, vocabularies, and pronunciation. A brief description of some of the main dialects found in the Tucson area is presented in Chapter 4. Vocabulary lists of Pochi Spanish and the Pachuco dialect will be found in Barker (1950) and a description of the derivation of the word in Sobarzo (1955).

With regard to linguistic terms, the writer has tried to limit himself to the use of only those found necessary to clarify the meaning of his descriptions in the task at hand. Following is a list, with definitions, of the main terms used.

Language: a system of arbitrary vocal symbols by means of which a social group cooperates (Bloch and Trager 1942).

Dialect: a local form of language which differs from the standard, or literary, form.

Standard: a language or dialect which conforms to the patterns of usage having the highest social prestige in the linguistic area in which it is used.

Substandard: a language or dialect which varies in form from the standard.

Bilingual: a person who has, first, approximately equal fluency in two languages; and second, who is making or has made in youth extensive and continuous use of both languages.

Linguistic form: a word, a part of a word, or a combination of words; thus, a word and a dialect are equally linguistic forms.

Phoneme: a minimum unit of distinctive sound feature in a language.

Linguistic structure: the way in which the phonemes and combinations of phonemes used as symbols in a language are arranged in relation to each other. Or, used in a broader sense, linguistic system.

Linguistic system: the languages and dialects used by an individual or group, defined in terms of their extent (range of languages, dialects), their parts (including vocabulary, syntax, tonal patterns, and individual variations in expression), and the frequency of their use in life situations (language usage).

Syntax: that aspect of linguistic structure which has to do with the way in which words are arranged in phrases in a language.

Sentence melody: the tonal patterns habitually followed by an individual in speaking a language or dialect.

Field Methods

The main field method used for this study was that of observation. The data emanating from this inquiry fall logically into three divisions which correspond to the three different levels on which this investigation was conducted.

On the lowest or least inclusive level are the data dealing with the language usage and social participation of twenty families of Mexican descent in Tucson. During the writer's residence in Tucson he had the opportunity to observe how people of Mexican descent talked and acted in the Mexican-American sections, in Anglo-American neighborhoods, and in the privacy of their own homes. The effort was made to observe individuals and families in a variety of situations and to see how their usage of Spanish and English compared with their actions in each case. To put people at their ease regarding his presence, the writer did not conduct formal interviews or take down conversations as they occurred. Rather, he attempted to become acquainted with people simply through casual and informal social and business contacts. In the Mexican neighborhood in which he lived he was known as a student who was interested in Mexican customs. As such he was not too obtrusive a figure, and was able to hear many conversations during which the participants took little or no notice of his presence.

On a slightly higher level are the data dealing with the language usage of formal and informal groups of Mexican-Americans in their social and economic relations in Tucson. At the beginning of his stay, and also at the end, the writer had a series of informal interviews with individuals prominent in Mexican and Anglo society in Tucson. The object of these interviews was not so much to obtain data on the subjects' language usage as it was to obtain background material on the languages and dialects used in Tucson and on the social structure and Mexican participation in the life of the town. These interviews were supplemented by others obtained by Getty (unpublished interview material) over a three-year period.

Finally, on the highest and most abstract level, are the data dealing with the cultural influences in Tucson life in relation to the family language usage of more than two hundred Mexican-American schoolchildren. These data were gathered through questionnaires of which there were two types. The first was a series of eighteen questions submitted to 277 sixth-grade schoolchildren by teachers or principals in five Tucson elementary schools while the writer was in the field in January and February 1946. The information sought in this questionnaire included data on the child's family, period of residence in Tucson, language usage, and cultural interests. This questionnaire was filled out by about two hundred Mexican pupils and about sixty Anglo pupils. The second questionnaire was far more limited in scope and number. It was designed simply to fill in blank spots in the writer's information on the family language usage of some of the subjects, and was sent out by mail after the writer had left the field. Out of a total of seven forms sent, six were returned with the information requested.

The aim in collecting data on these three levels was first, to provide the means of cross-checking the reliability of the data on the three levels and, second, to enable the forming of broader generalizations than could be made on the basis of data obtained on one level alone.

Technique of Recording Data

Throughout his stay in Tucson, the writer kept a diary of his activities, and also kept a file on the background and language usage of the families with which he became acquainted. These two sources were used to compile the records of family language usage contained in this thesis.

To clarify this technique of recording data, it should be pointed out that the writer's diary repre-sented an abstract of each day's events, usually recorded at the end of each day. The conversational data represent abstracts of conversations which the writer heard or in which he participated; the former were usually recorded on the day, or the day after, they were heard. In using these two sources to compile the data, the writer found that occasionally his memory would supply bits of information that were not contained in either of the two sources, and accordingly used them in the compilation. In a very few instances he relied on his memory alone to reconstruct a conversation-event to which he could find no reference in either the diary or file.

While the lack of detailed verbatim material, taken down on the spot at the moment of occurrence, may justly be considered a weakness in the field material, the writer did not attempt to get such verbatim reports for two reasons: first, the conversations usually were too rapid for accurate recording, and second, the writer did not want to spoil the spontaneity of a conversation by being seen taking notes on it. In a few instances, however, especially in the reporting of children's play, he was able to record, unobserved, conversational sequences as they occurred.

Chapter 3

SOCIOLOGICAL BACKGROUND—
TUCSON IN THE MID-1940s

Of Tucson's total population in the mid-1940s, a little more than one-fourth, or about twenty-five thousand persons, are of Mexican descent. Some of these people take little or no part in the life of the Mexican community but the vast majority, either because of family connections, residence, occupation, or social background, or a combination of these factors, are involved in it in one way or another. Since a knowledge of this community and of its relation to the Tucson social structure is vital to the present study, a brief outline of these basic sociological conditions and their effect in shaping the problem at hand will next be presented.

The most striking feature of Tucson's social structure is its division into two main parts—Anglo and Mexican. Without attempting to trace in detail the development of this division, we may say that it goes back at least to the beginning of the American occupation of this originally Mexican pueblo in the mid-1850s. While American authorities have never pursued a policy of deliberate segregation, there was, from the very earliest American settlement, a tendency for the Anglos to settle in the northern part of town and to leave the south very largely Mexican in composition. This tendency was reinforced after the coming of the Southern Pacific railroad from California in 1880, since new Anglo settlers preferred to live on higher ground on the north and east sides of town. By 1915, at the beginning of a new and heavy American influx, almost all the newcomers were settling on the east side of the tracks.

The Anglos immigrating to Tucson during the first half century of American sovereignty were almost without exception drawn from the upper and middle classes of people in other American cities. Many of these people were retired businessmen and their families; others were health seekers who could afford to spend at least a part of their time in the beneficial climate of Tucson. Lower-class people were not attracted to Tucson for there were in Tucson no large industries and the town already had an abundant supply of cheap Mexican and Indian labor. It is thus apparent that from the very start of Tucson's American occupation, the town's lower class has been drawn almost exclusively from its large Mexican population.

The exact delineation of Tucson's class structure is a separate problem, and is not within the scope of this thesis. However, on the basis of residence, occupation, and social participation, such main features as the above-mentioned division between the bulk of the Anglo and Mexican populations can be roughly outlined.

Anglo Neighborhoods and Social Organization

The Anglo population can be divided into four subgroups. The topmost of these is a small upper class made up of the descendants of "pioneer" American families who enjoy ownership of some of the leading business establishments, reside in the most exclusive neighborhoods, and command top social prestige in the town. A second group, clearly demarcated from the first, would appear to fit Lloyd Warner's description of an upper-middle class. Its members are leading business and professional men and their families who live in "high class" but not the "top" residential areas in the northeast part of town and who participate socially in all but a few exclusive organizations of the top group. Less distinctly set off from the second or upper-middle class is a lower-middle group composed of small merchants, clerks, and teachers in the public schools and their families. These people take part in some but not all of the organizations to which upper-middle-class people belong, and live in neighborhoods which, although generally still on the east side of the tracks, are composed of smaller and more modest homes. Finally, since World War II, Tucson has had the rudiments of a lower-class Anglo group composed of laborers and their families who came to Tucson from the Middle West to work in the town's war industries. Almost all the members of this lower-class group live on the south side of town.

On the basis of physical appearance as well as of the social evaluation of key informants, the various Anglo neighborhoods in Tucson may be divided roughly into four main groups corresponding to the above-suggested four socioeconomic classes of the Anglo population. As a background for our study of Tucson's Mexican-American minority, an attempt will now be made to describe in briefest outline some of the representative Anglo neighborhoods together with the kind of social organization which is found at the various Anglo socioeconomic levels.

When asked what they considered to be the top-ranking residential areas in Tucson, informants were unanimously agreed on three — El Encanto Estates and Colonia Solana on the east, and the Catalina Foothills Estates on the north side of town. As an afterthought, many informants also mentioned a high-class westside neighborhood known as "Snob Hollow" or "Paseo Redondo," but such mention always was accompanied by the statement that this area is on the decline (see map).

Snob Hollow is the oldest of these high-class residential areas of Tucson, and may be considered a prototype for the others. In size Snob Hollow is not large. It extends over a small basin some five or six square blocks in area, located just west of the old Placita, near the "Centro" of the old Mexican pueblo. To passersby looking down into this park-like residential area from Main Street, it offers a striking contrast to the tenement-like adobes of the crowded Centro. The curving avenues of Snob Hollow are bordered by tall shade trees and green lawns. Houses are set well back from the street, and often are half-hidden by luxuriant foliage. In style some of the houses seem to have borrowed from the conventions of the East and Middle West, while others have a Latin touch. Many of these are mansions with two stories and from ten to fifteen rooms, not counting outbuildings.

Snob Hollow's declining position is described by one informant:

Snob Hollow used to be the Number One area of Tucson. I believe it was the first subdivision to be established in Tucson with restrictions. Yes, years ago it was the topnotch area of Tucson, but it's disintegrating now. There are only a few of the old families that were the first families of Tucson. These included the A, B, C, D, E, and F families.

But they are all in social eclipse now. The elder C's were the social elite in their day, but the younger generation of C's run in a fast crowd. That whole area of Snob Hollow is now just an area of boarding houses. A lot of those big old houses are now full of roomers.

El Encanto Estates and Colonia Solana, the two neighborhoods most frequently mentioned as successors to Snob Hollow, occupy a connected area of about two square miles, a bit more than two miles due east of Tucson's central business section. The land here is slightly higher in elevation than the downtown area and is not so susceptible to dust storms as is the area near the flats of the Santa Cruz River. Added to these natural advantages are three man-made assets: first, the extensive grounds of the exclusive El Conquistador Hotel, which lies immediately east of El Encanto; second, the Tucson Municipal Golf Course which lies immediately east of Colonia Solana; and, third, Randolph Park, Tucson's largest playground, which borders Colonia Solana on the south.

In general appearance, it is hard to distinguish between El Encanto Estates and Colonia Solana. Both have pleasingly curved and paved avenues which afford excellent views of the mountains which surround Tucson. In both there is a preponderance of long, low, modern one-story houses, each set well back on an acre or two of carefully landscaped grounds. These houses are smaller than the mansions of Snob Hollow, and seem to average in size from about eight to twelve rooms. Many of them are Mexican or American Colonial in style, and all are designed to take full advantage of desert vistas. Interspersed among these one-story houses are a few two-story Mediterranean and pueblo-style houses, modern in construction but still not so large as those of Snob Hollow. Only in the extent of their development do El Encanto and Colonia Solana differ markedly from each other. While El Encanto is very well built up, only one corner of Colonia Solana has houses. The rest of its exclusive avenues wind in and out among the desert cacti.

Unlike the two neighborhoods just mentioned, the Catalina Foothills Estates, third of the top-ranking residential areas, lies outside the city limits and is separated from the town by about five miles of open desert. In area this subdivision includes about four square miles located on top of a series of mesas at the base of the mountains of the Coronado National Forest north of town. Perhaps the

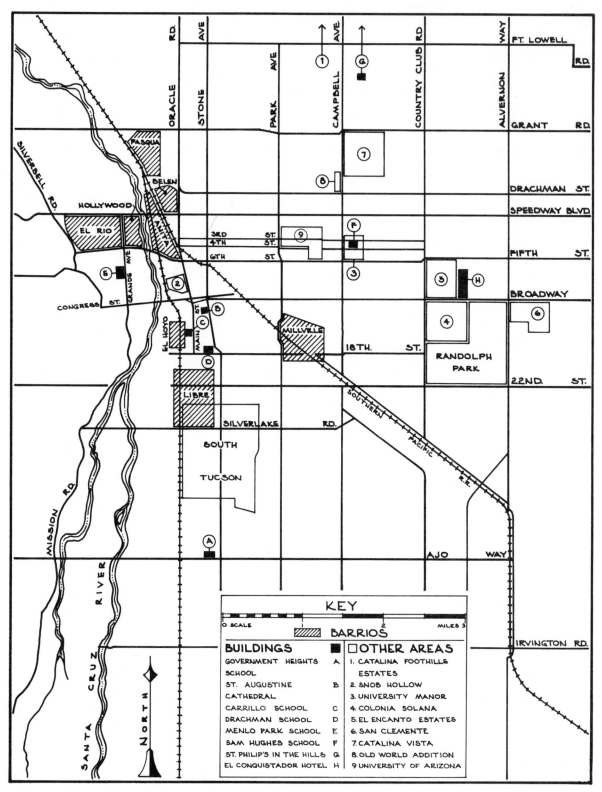

Tucson in the Mid-1940s

most distinctive feature of this neighborhood is its altitude. From its superior height, residents have unobstructed views not only of the mountains around Tucson but also can look down upon all other areas of the town itself. This natural asset seems to have had wide appeal for many wealthy eastern people who have chosen this site for their winter homes. The long low houses, corresponding in size to those of El Encanto, are frequently ranch style and are informal to the point of leaving almost untouched the natural shrubbery of the surrounding desert. Adding to the ranch effect are the wide areas of desert between the houses. The one part of the Foothills Estates where there seems to be a concentration of buildings is at its very entrance, where there are two or three studios, a fashionable restaurant, and the Episcopal Church of St. Philip's in the Hills.

While informants agreed that the three neighborhoods mentioned above were the prestige neighborhoods of Tucson, they differed as to the order in which these areas might be ranked. The ranking seemed to differ according to whether the informant placed money or social background as the chief criterion of social prestige. Thus, one informant, asked why she placed El Encanto and Colonia Solana first, replied that she based her judgment on "the money and social position" of the people living in these areas. In regard to the Catalina Foothills, the same informant remarked:

I guess most of that is still high class, and of course there are rather strict restrictions there. But there are plenty of people living out there who don't have the means that the people in El Encanto and Colonia Solana have.

Another informant reversed this order:

Well, I think that when El Encanto was first established it did contain the highest class people in Tucson, highest class in all respects, both in regard to money and education. But more recently people, and many of them local people, who have only money, have been moving into El Encanto. Many of these people who have moved into El Encanto recently are local men who have made good right here in Tucson; they are self-made men who have made their money right here. Now the people in the Foothills are to a large extent people who have come here from the east, and who have both money and education and background. They are eastern University men: Yale, Princeton, Cornell, Harvard, etc.

The second main group of Anglo residential areas includes San Clemente, Catalina Vista, University Manor, and the Old World Addition, all on the northeast side of town. The houses in these areas average from seven to nine rooms and are located on large, well-kept lots. The relation of these neighborhoods to the districts surrounding them has been described:

In the area north and east of the business district, there are one or two islands that stand out. The area known as University Manor is one island. In a rough way it might be considered to extend from Speedway to Sixth, and from Campbell to Country Club. But I would narrow it down to the area between Campbell and the Sam Hughes School along Third, Fourth, and Fifth Streets. That has some very nice homes in it. And, furthermore, it is solidly built in; it is the most solidly built-in area in Tucson.

The third main group of Anglo residential areas comprises most of the rest of the neighborhoods on the northeast side of town. The houses in these neighborhoods contain an average of four or five rooms. They are crowded together on thirty- or forty-foot lots and generally are of frame and stucco construction. In the words of one informant, these neighborhoods are "all a step lower than the areas we have been talking about — I guess you might say middle-class."

Another informant describes these neighborhoods:

The whole area between the University campus and the business district is going down in caliber. It is becoming an area of boarding and rooming houses interspersed with business establishments. You take the area east of the Grace Episcopal Church along Third Street, that was a fairly high class area not so long ago, at least high middle class. But as soon as the Tucson Mortuary was put in there at Third and Stone, across from the church, that whole area east of there dropped.

The fourth group of Anglo neighborhoods is made up largely of the Anglo residential areas south and west of the railroad tracks. In many of these areas streets are unpaved, there are no trees, and houses are small and scattered. In appearance, houses are of boxlike frame or stucco construction and average about four rooms. Vacant lots often are used to accommodate trailers.

From this brief description of Anglo neighborhoods and house types, it may be seen that Tucson's Anglo population is an extremely heterogeneous group, not only from the standpoint of wealth and occupation but from that of social background and origin. These divergencies are reflected in the kinds of Anglo social organization found in the Tucson area. Tucson's society might almost be described as a series of circles, sometimes tangential and sometimes overlapping, each with its own center of activity and its own system of prestige. One such circle, barely tangent to the others, would seem to be the group of wealthy eastern visitors. Another would seem to be that of the Tucson townspeople. A third circle, overlapping the second, might be described as that of the University group. A fourth circle, also overlapping the second, would seem to be the group of Midwestern health seekers.

To describe all of these circles would be far beyond the province of this thesis. Something should be said, however, concerning the social organization of the townspeople, since this group seems to be linked to the political and economic controls of the general Tucson community.

The townspeople who are considered to be socially at the top in Tucson form a small and exclusive set. The nucleus of this group is composed of descendants of some of the pioneer American families who have inherited and developed their family properties and businesses. The group also includes some wealthy Midwesterners who have settled in Tucson and identified themselves with town life over a period of years.

The exclusive character of this top group of townspeople is maintained through both formal and informal types of association. Most prominent among the formal organizations is the Board of Governors of the Episcopal Sanitarium, St. Luke's in the Desert. The leaders on this board generally are people who reside either in Snob Hollow or El Encanto Estates. When anyone is proposed for the board, the senior members immediately ask, "Who is she, and how long has she lived in Tucson?" The person selected must definitely have "identified herself" with Tucson. Other exclusive formal associations of the top group are the Junior League and the Saturday Morning Musical club. Other formal organizations of the top-ranking group are the Children's Home Board, the new Tucson Country Club, the Hunt Club (for fox-and-hounds hunting), and the Planned Parenthood Board.

Informal associations of the top group take the form of cocktail parties (for both men and women), teas, and elaborate luncheons (for women). Most of the entertaining is done in the homes, though some of the people are members of the Old Pueblo Club and El Rio Golf and Country Club. These clubs, which basically are men's organizations, are not so exclusive as the above-mentioned top women's associations; while the old families of American stock comprise the backbone of their membership, they also include a number of families who might be described in terms of wealth and background as "upper-middle class" in the Tucson community.

Many Tucson associations, of course, are not limited in membership to persons of any one socioeconomic level. Perhaps the organization having the widest social range is the American Legion, whose membership is so wide and diversified that it has been split up into a number of separate posts. Second only to the Legion in social range is the Chamber of Commerce. Its membership of 850 ranges from owners of small one-man shops to the town's leaders in business and civic affairs. The Tucson Women's Club seems to have a similarly broad range, although relatively few of its members could be described as upper class.

Some formal associations may be ranked into "hierarchies" corresponding roughly to various levels of the class system. (The term "hierarchies" is used here in a loose sense and does not imply that the various organizations included are under a single control.) Among service clubs, for example, Rotary is at the top, although its roster includes many members whose social position could be described as upper-middle class. Competing for second place in this hierarchy are the Lions and Kiwanis clubs, whose members occupy high but not top positions in business and professional circles. Other service clubs draw more heavily on men of lower-middle-class status for their membership. Among fraternal organizations, the Masons are at the top although here, again, the roster covers a wide range of the class system. The Elks and Knights of Columbus seem to be composed largely of individuals having middle-class status, a point of special interest since the Knights of Columbus membership includes several persons of Mexican descent who might be considered "upper class" in the Mexican, but not the Anglo, community.

Tucson's Protestant churches also may be

described as a kind of social hierarchy. At the top is the small Episcopal Church of St. Philip's in the Hills situated at the entrance to the Catalina Foothills Estates. St. Philip's has a former eastern prelate as its rector. Slightly lower in prestige, and covering a much broader social range is another Episcopal institution, Grace Church. Approximately equal in rank to Grace Church is the large First Congregational Church, which has 400 covenantors and a constituency of 800. Members of this church seem to be largely upper-middle class in status and live on the east side of town. According to the minister, a spot map would place 90 percent of the members on the east side of the University. A few of the church's oldest members, however, live in Snob Hollow. Other churches catering to people of middle-class status are the University Methodist Church, the Lutheran Church, and the Baptist Church. Of these, the first (Northern) Baptist Church seems to have the widest social range and to exert a strong moral influence in community affairs. Finally, there are on the south and west fringes of town a group of evangelical churches whose membership may be described as lower class. Many of the members of these institutions are families from the "Bible Belt" of Oklahoma, Arkansas, and Missouri, who have come to Tucson only since the beginning of the 1940s.

To summarize this sketchy and synoptic presentation of social organization in the Anglo community, we may say that the pattern of Anglo social life in Tucson is not rigid, but rather seems to be remarkably flexible, due to the constant influx of new residents. Only in the topmost social group are there strong bars as to what Anglo may belong; and even here it is not necessary to have been born in Tucson in order to participate. Social background is an asset to anyone desiring to enter this group, but it seems evident that obscure backgrounds can be overlooked in the cases of Anglos who rank high in wealth and occupational status. With respect to persons of Mexican descent, however, our evidence seems to indicate a somewhat different picture, and it is to this evidence that we now turn.

Mexican Neighborhoods and Social Organization

The railroad tracks are significant not only in the division between the Anglo and Mexican communities, but also in the structure of the Mexican community itself. The bulk of the Mexican population lives on the westerly side of the main Southern Pacific tracks, which bisect the city diagonally from northwest to southeast. A comparative handful of Mexican people, however, lives among the Anglo-Americans on the east side of the tracks. Practically all of the people on the west side have some share in the life of the Mexican community. A few of those living on the east side also take part in the life of the Mexican community but their participation is relatively slight, and they are important to this community more as eminent figureheads than as leaders.

Besides this basic division of east and west, there are other geographic divisions that further differentiate those parts of the Mexican population living on the west side. There is first of all the "Centro" or nucleus of the old Mexican pueblo, in the downtown section of the city where many Mexican families still live. Then, radiating outward both to the northwest and south, are the various barrios or neighborhoods. Those to the south include Barrio Libre and Barrio Millville, and to the northwest, Barrio Anita, and the newer Hollywood and El Rio, and Barrio Pascua and Belen, this latter adjoining the village of Pascua.

According to Getty's and the writer's observations, as well as the testimony of our informants, the barrios are primarily geographic units and do not differ sharply from one another in social composition. However, there is considerable evidence that the barrios are socially distinct neighborhoods, each with its peculiar characteristics. It seems significant, first of all, that the younger generation is familiar with the barrio names and the areas occupied by each. It also is evident that the economic level of the people in the El Rio Barrio, and to a lesser extent in the Hollywood Barrio, is slightly higher than that of some of the older barrios, since these two relatively new barrios have been populated largely by people from the other barrios who have been enterprising enough to change their status from one of tenants in the overcrowded older sections of town to that of owners of small adobe houses in the new neighborhoods. At the same time it is worth noting that Getty's (1943–46) study indicates that differences in occupational statuses represented in the various barrios are slight. Finally, there is some evidence of barrio rivalry and barrio solidarity among the younger generation. For many years, for example, there has been friction between gangs of boys from Barrio Libre and Barrio Anita, and also between Barrio Libre and the "Centro." More recently, the writer was informed that there has been friction between the Barrio Libre boys and those of El Rio, due to an "invasion" of the latter's territory by the former.

From the standpoint of the present study, by far the most important of the geographic divisions mentioned above is that between the east and west. This sharp difference is immediately apparent in a comparison of house types and streets in the two parts of town. The houses of the barrios are generally small boxlike adobe structures, often with no inside plumbing or even cement floors. The yard surrounding the house usually is bare, with perhaps a few straggling patches of grass fronting the street. In the back, there is generally a wood pile, outhouse, and chicken shed. In contrast, the houses of people of Mexican descent on the east side of town are much larger, patterned after American standards, with inside bathrooms, gas or electric appliances for heating and cooking, and with pleasingly landscaped yards. Also, unlike the rough and dusty streets commonly found on the west, the streets on the east side are far more frequently paved and tree-lined.

The above physical differences mirror differences in the socioeconomic statuses of Mexican people living in the two areas. In occupation, the people of the barrios are generally unskilled or skilled laborers, tradesmen, small shop owners, or clerical assistants. On the other hand, those people of Mexican descent who live on the east side are generally either professional people — owners of medium- or large-sized business enterprises — or white-collar employees having responsible positions in such enterprises.

Important as the railroad tracks are, however, they are by no means a hard and fast dividing line of social class in the Mexican community. Many people of considerable social distinction still live on the west side of town. Included in this group are many younger members of the exclusive Club Latino, whose roster supposedly is limited to Tucson's sixty Mexican families of highest social prestige. Some of these people have moved from the crowded central sections of the city to the new residential locations in the south part of town. Despite its position west of the railroad tracks, South Tucson has an attractive residential area in which homes of Mexicans and Anglos are inter-spersed, and which compares favorably with lower-middle-class Anglo neighborhoods on the east side of the city.

As between the barrios themselves, the contrasts are much less sharp than those between the east and west. The most marked differences are those between the unplastered shacklike adobe huts in the southwest part of the Barrio Libre, along the Santa Cruz River, and the neatly plastered and painted adobe or concrete-block houses of El Rio. These differences, again, reflect differences in socio-economic statuses. The people in the southwest part of Barrio Libre are mainly families of migrant workers or day laborers, and represent the lowest economic level in the city. In the other barrios, and especially El Rio, most of the families have one or more members with steady year-round jobs either as unskilled or semiskilled laborers. As we have already noted, these other neighborhoods also have a fair scattering of skilled laborers, clerical assistants, and small shop-owners.

In terms of socioeconomic class, then, there seem to be at least five groups represented in the Mexican community in Tucson (see Table 1). The highest or "upper" of these may be said to be composed of those wealthy "Old Families" of Mexican descent who live on the east side of the railroad tracks. The lowest is the group of unskilled migrant worker families in the southwest, while in between are, first, the steadily employed unskilled or semi-skilled laboring groups, who might be regarded as a sort of "upper-lower" class and, second, the group of skilled laborers, tradesmen, clerical workers, and small merchants who comprise what might be called the Mexican community's middle class and, third, that less prominent and less well established younger element of the upper group whose members live on both sides of the tracks, and which might be said to compose the Mexican community's "lower-upper" class.

Two other important divisions — those of age-group and national origin — cross cut the divisions of geography and social class in the Mexican community. From the estimate of informants, government reports, and the writer's own survey, it seems evident that about half of the Mexican residents of forty years of age or older are immigrants from Mexico. Most of these people came to the United States in the two decades following the collapse of the Díaz regime in 1910, and permanent immigration since then has been relatively slight. The result

Table 1
CHARACTERISTICS OF TWENTY FAMILIES

NAME OF FAMILY	COMPOSITION OF FAMILY				OCCUPATION OF EMPLOYED ADULTS	IMMIGRATION STATUS **		SOCIOECONOMIC RELATIONSHIPS OF FAMILY			PLACE IN SOCIAL HIERARCHY OF MEXICAN COMMUNITY		
WEST SIDE (Mexican Barrios)	F*	M*	C	Other		F	M	Church	Anglo	Mexican	Lower	Middle	Upper
Uno	x	x	4		labor	US	US	weak	lim	lim	x →x	x	
Tres		x	3	uncle, md, h	3/labor		US	weak		weak	x		
Diez	(away)	x	3	aunt, uncle	labor		US	lim	lim		x →x	x	
Once	x	x	6	gm	labor	Mexico	Mexico	lim		weak		x	
Doce	x	x	8	gm	labor	US	Mexico	weak		lim	x		
Trece	x	x	4		municipal	(Mexico)	US	strong		lim		x	
Catorce		x	5	md, h	domestic		US	none		lim	x		
Quince	x	x	1		labor	US	(Mexico)	none	lim			x	
Veinte	x	x	3		business	(Mexico)	US	weak	lim	lim		x	
Treinta	x	x	7		business	Mexico	Mexico	none	strong	lim		x	
Cuarenta		x	3	gm	business	(Mexico)		none		lim	x		
INTERMEDIATE AREA (Mexican Barrios)													
Cincuenta	(gf)	x	2	md, h	2/labor	US		none		lim		x	
Seis	x	x	3	aunt	business	US	US	none		strong		x	
Ocho	x	x	2		business	US	US	none		strong		x	
EAST SIDE (East of Railroad)													
Sesenta		x	4		4/educa.		Mexico		lim	lim		x	
Dos	x	x	1		municipal	US		none	strong				x
Cuatro	x	x	2		business	US	S. Amer.	none	lim	strong			x
Cinco	x	x	2		educa.	US	US	none	lim			x	
Siete	(away)	x	1		secretarial		Mexico	none		lim		x	
Nueve	(gf)	(gm)	3		business	Mexico	US	none	strong	lim			x

Abbreviations
C   Children
F   Father
gm   grandmother
gf   grandfather
h   Husband
lim   limited
M   Mother
md   married daughter

* Terms in parentheses = surrogate parents

** US = first generation born in US.
(Mexico) = from Mexico when younger than 18.
Mexico = from Mexico when older than 18.

has been to increase the separateness of this group not only as immigrants but as an age group. In the Hollywood Barrio, for example, a majority of the adults who are forty years of age are immigrants from the Mexican state of Sonora.

Besides this immigrant group, there are several other groups that may be distinguished on the basis of age and nationality. The most obvious of these is the so-called "Old Families" group, made up of descendants of families prominent in Tucson life during the pioneer period of American occupation. Many of the members of this group, by reason of their prestige and association with the development of Tucson, still hold considerable influence in the Tucson Mexican community. They also are highly respected in the Anglo community, although they do not participate as actively in its social life as they do in its business enterprises. Their position as Tucson residents seems to be unique in that, while they are nominally members of both communities, they are not socially integrated with either. They are inclined to keep themselves aloof from the large immigrant group which is the core of the Mexican community, and at the same time they have very few social relations with the upper-middle-class Anglo group which corresponds socially with their own status (see Table 1).

A third group, much larger than these others, is composed of American-born adults whose families, though not so prominent as the "Old Families," were Tucson families and reared their children in the city under the dominance of American educational, economic, and governmental controls. The bulk of these people, whom we may call "Pochis" — a word used in a more limited sense to refer to American-born Mexicans of California, but also to denote any American-born person of Mexican descent — are members of the Tucson Mexican community, but some of them resent the subordinate social and occupational position which this membership imposes. This dissatisfaction is increased by the fact that unlike the immigrants, who are culturally cut off from the Anglos, the American-born Mexican of Tucson is culturally more like the Anglo than like the immigrant, but as a "Mexican" he cannot achieve the goals which the Anglo community sets up for its own members. The result is that some of the Pochis are striving to dissociate themselves from the Mexican community in order to gain acceptance and mobility as members of the dominant Anglo group.

A fourth major age-nationality grouping is that of the school-age children of Mexican descent. Almost without exception, these children are American-born, and most of them are between the ages of six and sixteen. Besides their age and nationality status, they have in common a background which is more or less bicultural. Almost all are of Catholic parentage, and within their families the traditions of Mexican religio-familial observances continue largely unbroken. They attend Mass and the "doctrina" or catechism class, celebrate baptisms, weddings, and Saints' days in much the same manner as their ancestors did. It is only through their relatively impersonal contacts with the Anglo community that Anglo culture enters into their lives. The urban life of Tucson is dominantly Anglo-American, and on this level Anglo culture competes with Mexican culture for the attention of the younger generation. Anglo standards of dress, business life, and recreation are the accepted for Tucson residents, and Tucson children are expected to conform. For amusement, a youth of Mexican descent may attend a Mexican movie but there are four times as many American shows from which he may choose. Also, the areas of competition of Mexican and United States culture are not limited to the downtown districts, for through the radio, the comic strip, and the popular magazines, United States culture now penetrates into homes in even the most solidly Mexican neighborhoods.

Within the school-age group there are, of course, several subdivisions which it may be well to mention at this time. The children of the "Old Families" differ to some degree in cultural background from those of other American-born families, and these in turn differ from families of the immigrant group. The problems of adjustment are correspondingly different for each of these subgroups. The children of "Old Families," living as they do on the east side of town, must meet the standards of Anglo children from the very beginning of neighborhood life. Even the Catholic parochial schools on the east side have more Anglo than Mexican pupils. The children of American-born Mexicans are faced with the problem of reconciling two conflicting standards of behavior — Mexican and American — and they find themselves surrounded by a cultural atmosphere in the barrios which is strongly at variance with the goals which their Pochi parents have fostered in their own homes. The children of immigrants, finally, have the most serious problem of all, since the cultural background and equipment of their own parents differ most sharply from the general standards of the dominant Anglo community.

Relative Social Position of the Mexican Community in Tucson

From the above brief description of its main divisions, it is possible to have some idea of the position of the Mexican community in the Tucson social system. Stated in briefest terms, this position is one of subordination in the Tucson social structure. Since this social subordination constitutes one of the conditions most basic in testing an evaluation of the hypotheses of this inquiry, a further clarification of this condition now seems in order.

There are three main lines of evidence which help to define the subordinate relation of the Mexican community within the Tucson social structure. The first of these may be described as the ecological or human-use-of-the-land situation in the Tucson area. As we have already noted, Tucson is divided into a series of neighborhoods which lie some to the east and some to the west of the diagonal swath cut by the Southern Pacific tracks (see map). In the early years, following the coming of the railroad in 1880, there was little or no social distinction between neighborhoods on the left and right sides of the tracks. Paseo Redondo — the "Snob Hollow" Anglo neighborhood of highest social prestige — was actually established on the west side of the tracks, and while many Mexicans of relatively modest social standing lived on the east side, the "Old Families" built imposing mansions on the west. The influx of a large and well-to-do Anglo population in the early years of the present century brought sharp changes in this situation. Following the establishment of the University of Arizona and the laying out of new and modern residential sections on higher ground in the east, this part of town became gradually mainly Anglo in composition. Rising rents and land prices led many Mexican families to sell their holdings on the east side and move to the west part of town. As these older Mexican sections became overcrowded, the Mexican people were forced to look even farther west rather than east for a place to go. The cheapest and least desirable vacant land in town lay along the Santa Cruz River bottom on the west, and it was to this area that the Mexican population now overflowed and put up their boxlike adobe cabins.

Now, more than sixty years after the coming of the railroad, almost all the Tucson neighborhoods can be ranked ecologically according to whether they are on the east or west side of the tracks. With the exception of Snob Hollow, all the economically first-class neighborhoods are on the east side and with no exception all of these first-class neighborhoods are dominantly Anglo.

As a way of defining more precisely the ecological positions of the Mexicans, we may note their distribution in the various Anglo neighborhoods (see Table 1). The four districts of Tucson which have the highest social ranking are Snob Hollow, El Encanto Estates, Colonia Solana, and the Catalina Foothills Estates. As far as is known to the writer, there is only one family of Mexican descent living in any of these four neighborhoods, although four other families live east of the railroad tracks in other localities. This fact appears more striking when it is recalled that some of the city's Mexican residents are financially very well off and could afford to maintain a home in one of these "exclusive" districts if they so chose.

To locate the homes of these wealthy Mexicans, we have to examine the Anglo neighborhoods that are ecologically between the top four mentioned above and the older and least desirable Anglo sections. These intermediate neighborhoods are located, with one exception, in the northeast part of town, near the University of Arizona campus. Within these areas are interspersed the homes of most of Tucson's more prosperous Mexican families. These families, of course, comprise a very small minority of Tucson's Mexican population and

an even smaller minority — probably less than 10 percent — of the neighborhoods in which they live.

Slightly below the standard of these intermediate areas, yet above that of the barrios, is the new residential area of the separately incorporated town of South Tucson, bounded by Twenty-fifth and Fortieth Streets on the north and south, respectively, and south Eleventh and First Avenues on the west and east, respectively. Here lives a larger proportion of Mexican-Americans of considerable business and professional standing, who though not so wealthy as some of the "Old Families," have sufficient means to maintain homes that compare favorably with Anglo middle-class standards. While the Anglos here are not so numerically superior as in other intermediate neighborhoods, they do comprise a substantial majority of the area. The Government Heights School, which serves this district, has an enrollment of 60 percent Anglo and 40 percent Mexican children.

With the above ecological picture in mind, we may now turn to the second main line of evidence of the relative position of the Mexican community — namely, information on the participation of individuals of Mexican descent in the general social life of Tucson (see Table 1). Let us examine first the membership in some formal social organizations which are top-ranking in Tucson society. Our informants were agreed that three such organizations are first, the Board of Visitors of the Charity Sanitarium, known as St. Luke's in the Desert; second, the Saturday Morning Musical club, and, third, the Junior League. In the first two, there are no members of Mexican descent. In the Junior League, there is one member who is the wife of a descendant of one of the "Old Families." Membership in the League is understood to be restricted to Anglos, excepting in a very few cases like the above, in which an Anglo girl of good standing marries a Mexican of high standing. According to one of our most reliable informants, the bars would not be let down in an "opposite" situation — one in which a socially prominent Anglo married a Mexican girl of high standing.

One of the main functions of the St. Luke's Board is its annual sponsoring of the Baile de las Flores, for many years the outstanding event of Tucson's social calendar. While the direction of this event is jealously guarded by the board members, participation in it is open to people of lesser social prestige. On this level, which includes the committees on arrangements, several of the "Old Families" of Mexican descent are active. With the exception of wartime Red Cross work, this is the only instance known to the writer in which people of the highest rank in the Mexican community come into direct social contact with the highest social group of Anglos.

On a slightly lower social level, there are at least two prominent Tucson social organizations with a fair number of members of Mexican descent. These are the Old Pueblo Club and El Rio Golf and Country Club. Some of the Tucson "Four Hundred" or top social group belong to these clubs, but this top group functions independently of them, since most of the entertaining in this highest Tucson social class is carried on in the homes of the members. This entertaining takes the form of cocktail parties for men and women, and teas and elaborate luncheons for women. The Mexican members of the Old Pueblo and El Rio clubs do not participate in these affairs, but tend, rather, to form their own cliques.

In the above notes on upper-class social life, enough has been said to indicate that the top social class in the Mexican community does not attain to the social level of the top Anglo group. The Mexican upper class tends more nearly to be the social equivalent of what might be described as the Anglo upper-middle class. Further evidence on this may be seen in the fact that the Tucson hotels and bars which are patronized by people in the upper-middle Anglo social circles also are patronized by the upper-class Mexicans, though on a far more limited scale.

Turning now to our third main line of evidence, on the occupational status of Anglos and Mexicans, we find a similar situation (see Table 1). Tucson has several businessmen of Mexican descent who occupy outstanding positions in the economic life of the city. One is the proprietor of one of the city's largest department stores, and another owns and operates a chain of drug stores. But while these individuals are economically on a par with the town's top Anglo businessmen, they constitute only a very small fraction of Tucson's economic leadership. Moreover, in civic affairs, they tend to assume subordinate positions rather than to seize the initiative. In the Chamber of Commerce, they are active on committees but not as directors or president. They are not represented on the board of trustees

of such institutions as the Y.M.C.A. or Y.W.C.A., the University of Arizona, or the Tucson Medical Center. In the municipal government they are represented by one councilman but not by the mayor or the powers behind his administration.

The small proportion of Mexicans to Anglos in Tucson's upper economic brackets is further illustrated by those in the ranks of Tucson's professional men. Whereas, according to the population figures, we should expect approximately one-fourth of Tucson's professional people to be of Mexican descent, actually the fraction is closer to one-fortieth. Out of over 125 physicians practicing in Tucson, only 3 are known to the writer to be of Mexican descent. Similarly, figures obtained from a study of the Tucson City Directory by Getty show that out of 197 practicing attorneys, there are only 4 who are Mexican, and of 30 dentists, only 1 is Mexican. Comparisons in other professional fields are equally striking; University professors: Anglo, 215, Mexican, 1; school principals: Anglo, 31, Mexican, 1; schoolteachers: Anglo, 478, Mexican, 11; county officials: Anglo, 36, Mexican, 2; city officials: Anglo, 40, Mexican, 3; building contractors: Anglo, 139, Mexican, 7; social workers: Anglo, 10, Mexican, 2.

As we go down the occupation ladder, the proportion of Mexicans to Anglos shows a proportional increase. Among small merchants, especially those serving its own population, the Mexican element is well represented. There also is a good-sized group of skilled laborers, such as mechanics, bricklayers, plasterers, taxi drivers, pipe fitters in the Southern Pacific shops, and, during World War II, in aircraft manufacture. On the level of unskilled labor, the proportion of Mexicans to Anglos is far greater. Goodman (1942) estimated that 75 percent of the total Mexican population is engaged in unskilled or semiskilled labor. The largest single source of work is the Southern Pacific railroad. Many Mexican laborers also are employed in city and county street work and as gardeners and domestic help. There is still one lower bracket — that of seasonal labor — and this group is practically entirely Mexican. The families who subsist on this kind of work — mainly cotton picking — are on the lowest economic level in Tucson.

Summarizing these three lines of evidence, we reach the following tentative conclusions as to the relative position of the Mexican community in the social structure of Tucson:

The class which is socially highest in the Mexican community is not represented, except for one family, in the four most exclusive Tucson residential neighborhoods, nor in the three most exclusive social groups, and only to a very limited extent in the top occupational bracket of the city. However, the members of the class do live in upper-middle-class Anglo neighborhoods, take part in upper-middle-class social activities, frequent hotels and bars patronized by upper-middle-class Anglos, and have an active subordinate role in civic affairs. We therefore conclude that the upper class in the Mexican community is the social equivalent of the upper-middle class in the general social structure of Tucson.

The class which is second highest in the Mexican community, composed of young executives and salesmen of good income, has its residences mainly in lower-middle-class Anglo neighborhoods. This group has its own exclusive social organization, the Club Latino, which is accorded the treatment of an upper-middle-class Anglo social group in the Anglo daily press. However, in wealth and occupational status, this group does not attain to the upper-middle level. Its status corresponds most closely to that of the lower-middle-class Anglo group, but there is little to prevent members who become more influential in the business life of the city from reaching upper-middle status.

The class ranking third in the Mexican community, made up of merchants and small shop owners, lives mainly in Mexican neighborhoods which by Anglo standards are rated as either lower-middle or upper-lower. The main organization of this group is the exclusive Club Anahuac which originally was intended to be a Mexican-American Chamber of Commerce. While the social prestige of this group in Tucson and in the Mexican community is considerably less than that of the Club Latino group, members are economically on a par with those in the second group. Their status, therefore, may be described as the equivalent of lower-middle class in the Anglo community, with the exception that unlike members of this group, their immigrant status prevents them from obtaining further upward mobility.

The fourth-ranking class in the Mexican community, composed of skilled and unskilled laborers having steady employment, live mainly in the Mexican barrios or in the poorer sections of South Tucson. Until World War II, this group had no parallel in the Anglo community, but with the migration of the lower-class white laboring men from the southern states, these Mexicans found themselves on a par with Tucson's lower-class Anglo group.

The fifth-ranking class of the Mexican community, that of its migratory workers, still has no parallel in the Anglo community and can be compared only with the lowest Negro group, together with which it comprises Tucson's lower class.

Types of Cultural Background in the Mexican Population

With the above picture of Tucson's social structure in mind, let us turn now to a brief consideration of another basic condition — the types of cultural background found among the Mexicans in Tucson. As we have seen in our discussion of school-aged children of Mexican descent, the bulk of the Mexican population is separated not only socially but culturally from the Anglo population. By this is meant that the Mexicans of Tucson, in contrast to the Anglos, have an element in their cultural heritage and upbringing which is entirely foreign to the Anglos. Yet, to some extent, they do take on the Anglo culture. In effect, the Mexicans are bicultural.

This bicultural background is found in varying degree among all elements of the Mexican population, excepting only the very recent immigrants. It may be considered as consisting of two main levels or fields. On one — the intimate level of family relations and religious activity — Mexican cultural interests are dominant. In the other — the more impersonal level of urban life — American cultural interests compete with Mexican cultural interests for their attention. The competition between cultures is intensified by Tucson's position on the main highway to Mexico, just 60 miles from the Mexican border.

The relative strength of these two cultural elements in any given family seems to vary according to the family's length of residence in the United States. The strongest cultural links with Mexico are found in the families of immigrants. In Tucson, there are more than two thousand immigrants who have taken up permanent residence. The influence of these individuals in imparting Mexican culture to their children and grandchildren is of course an important one, and marks their families as belonging to a different category than those of the Pochis — Mexican-Americans born in the United States.

The Tucson Pochis themselves may be divided into those of the first American-born generation (F_1), and those of the succeeding American-born generations. Most Tucson Pochis, including leading members of the "Old Families," are F_1, but there are probably several hundred adults of succeeding generations.

In view of the social and cultural diversity of the Mexicans in Tucson, one may well ask whether the mere fact of being "Mexican" is a handicap to an individual desiring to advance himself in Tucson society. The answer to this question is again a separate problem and is being made the subject of a special study by Getty. Enough evidence has been collected, however, to warrant the following statement: While there is no outright legally recognized segregation or discrimination against individuals of Mexican descent in Tucson, the label "Mexican" as applied to individuals living in Tucson carries an unfavorable connotation in any upper-class Anglo social circle. A definite indication of this may be found in the unwritten employment policies of numerous business concerns, in the membership restrictions of various Anglo upper-class social groups, and even in some of the student activities at the University of Arizona.

Further evidence along this line may be seen in the fact that some persons of Mexican descent in Tucson prefer to be known as "Spanish-Americans." This term has a much higher social prestige among Anglos than the term "Mexican," for while an Anglo will hesitate to refer to a friend of Mexi-

can descent as a "Mexican," he will have no compunction in speaking of him as a "Spanish-American." Generally speaking, when an individual lives in the barrios on the west side of town he is "Mexican," but when he moves to the east side he becomes a "Spanish-American" in Anglo eyes. For a "Mexican" the opportunity for upward social mobility in Tucson is definitely limited. To the writer's knowledge, there are no Mexican immigrants who have achieved upper-middle-class status in Tucson, although there are several who are on this level economically. (This, clearly, does not include second-, third-, or fourth-generation immigrants. See Table 1.) On the other hand, there is almost no limit to the upward social progress of the "Spanish-American." Thus it frequently happens that an individual of Mexican descent interested in improving his social status in Tucson will disassociate himself as much as possible from the Tucson Mexican community. This disassociation is accomplished, first, through a change in occupational status, in which the individual is promoted to a type of job in which he has no Mexican co-workers; second, through a change from a Mexican to an Anglo neighborhood; third, through a change from Mexican to Anglo religious and secular organizations; and, fourth, as we shall see, through changes in language usage. The result is that potential leaders of the Mexican community are absorbed into the Anglo group as Spanish-Americans just at the point when they might otherwise be of great service to their own group.

Chapter 4

LANGUAGE USAGE AND BACKGROUND

Material on the cultural interests and social participation of the twenty families chosen for study in this inquiry, supplemented by information derived from a questionnaire (see Chapter 2) for the families of more than 200 Mexican school-children in Tucson (see Tables 1, 2, and 3), indicates that there is little or no direct relation between the extent of the habitual use of Spanish in the family, on the one hand, and the extent of the social participation in the Mexican community, on the other. Moreover, investigation has revealed wide variations in linguistic and other social behavior even within the family unit. The most that can be said is that there is some correlation between the extent that Spanish is spoken in the family and (a) the neighborhood in which the family lives, and (b) the extent of the family's contacts with Spanish-speaking people.

It is important in this connection to distinguish between "language habits" and "language usage" as defined in this thesis. Language habits are simply the structural framework on which the study of language usage is conducted. Variations in usage cannot be understood or analyzed unless they are placed in relationship to the language habits of the individual or family in question. The fact that a given individual speaks Spanish entirely with his family is of no special significance in itself. Neither is the bald quantitative statement that children in the family speak half Spanish and half English to each other. When it is found that one of these individuals consistently favors English in his family in the presence of Spanish-speaking Anglos, however, we begin to get evidence of the relation of the individual's usage to his reaction to the dominant culture. When we find that the children of this individual refuse to use *pochismos* — Hispanicized-English words — in their speech because they and their parents regard such words as vulgar, we have further evidence along the line of this family's relation to the ethnic culture. It is the variation of individual linguistic responses in a variety of life situations that is our chief concern in this thesis. An attempt has been made to summarize some of

these variations of response within family units (see Table 3).

Four main variants of Spanish are spoken in Tucson. These are, considered in the order of their popularity, first, southern Arizona Spanish; second, standard Mexican; third, Pachuco; and fourth, the Yaqui dialect of Spanish. Since this last has only about eight hundred speakers in the Tucson area, and since we are not concerned with this group in the present study, our discussion will be limited to the other three dialects.

Southern Arizona Spanish has many points in common with the type of Spanish spoken by the Hispano-American of New Mexico (Post 1934). Older speakers of both dialects use many archaic forms that were brought to the New World during the sixteenth and seventeenth centuries, and which, due to the isolation of these speakers, have changed in locally limited ways, and have not been subject to the leveling effect of the standard language. Examples of the more common of these old forms include *binido* for *venido* (past participle of *venir,* to come), and *durmir* and *durmido* for *dormir* (to sleep) and *dormido*. Other similar forms are described by Hills (Henríquez Ureña 1938).

The southern Arizona dialect seems to have retained fewer of these old forms than has the dialect of New Mexico. Perhaps one reason for this is that Tucson children study standard Spanish in high school, junior high, and, since the spring of 1946, in grammar school. In their school Spanish, the children are being taught to substitute the standard forms for the old ones. Another point is that Tucson, located on direct rail and road routes to Mexico City, is less isolated from Mexico than many of the New Mexican communities.

Besides its archaic forms, another outstanding characteristic of southern Arizona Spanish is its heavy use of pochismos (Barker 1950). These forms are used most frequently by younger speakers, but older persons are by no means free of them. Not only words, but expressions, are borrowed and transposed by young and old alike. A priest told the writer that children making confession to him often told him that they had "hablado para atrás" (talked back to) their elders. A teacher of Mexican descent said she sometimes used the expression "me agarró el chivo" (he got my goat). Joe Uno, fixing a window-lever on his car, told the writer "está fuera de orden" (it's out of order). And old Grandpa Cincuenta wrote in a letter to the author "tubieron muy buen tiempo" (they had a very good time).

A third and increasingly prominent characteristic of southern Arizona Spanish is the tendency of its speakers to rely almost entirely on the familiar verb endings (second person) even though they may never have seen the person to whom they are speaking. This is especially true among younger speakers. A boy goes up to a soft-drink stand, for example, and asks "Qué tienes?" (what hast thou) although he may never have seen the girl who waits on him. The girl, in turn, may ask the customer "Qué quieres?" (what wishest thou). Discussing this same tendency on the part of the younger speakers of another dialect, Trager (1941) offers the explanation that children do not use the polite forms for the simple reason that their parents failed to teach them; when the children are the right age to learn these forms, they go to school and learn the American polite forms instead.

A fourth major characteristic of southern Arizona Spanish is its similarity to the Spanish of the northern part of the state of Sonora, Mexico. Speakers of southern Arizona Spanish have a pronounced sentence melody, or *sonsonete,* which is very similar to that of northern Sonora. This sentence melody is so firmly established as a linguistic pattern that Tucson children of Mexican descent frequently carry it over into their English. The main differences in the Spanish of the two areas seem to be (1) the much greater use in southern Arizona Spanish of Hispanicized English words or pochismos, (2) the greater use in Sonora of polite forms, and (3) the wider substitution in Sonora of standard forms in place of archaic words and expressions. The writer's informants seem to agree that these differences could be explained largely in terms of language training in school and especially in the family. In Sonora, for example, the use of many archaic forms seems to be limited to lower-class, uneducated people, while in southern Arizona they are more widely distributed.

To describe the type of standard Spanish spoken in Tucson as Mexican Spanish is perhaps an oversimplification, since the Republic of Mexico seems to be divided into at least five main dialect areas. The northern Sonora area we have described may perhaps be regarded as a subregion of one of these major areas, the *norteño.* Four other areas, each of which is characterized by similarly distinct differences in accent and vocabulary, are outlined by the Mexican linguist Henríquez Ureña (1938: xvii–xx), as the central area, or *el centro,* comprising the highlands of central Mexico; the south including Morelos, Guerrero, and Oaxaca; the Mexican Gulf coast or *costeño,* comprising Tamaulipas, Vera Cruz, Tabasco, and Campeche; and the region of Yucatan.

Of these five areas, the central one is the one that might best be described as the standard of Mexico, since it is the area in which is situated Mexico City, the capital, and, accordingly, the one which enjoys the greatest prestige. Of course, the Spanish of Mexico City has many features in common with the Spanish of the Mexican provinces, which together distinguish Mexican Spanish from the Castilian Spanish of Spain. Perhaps the chief ones of these are "yeísmo," the lack of distinction between the *ll* and *y;* "seseo," failure to distinguish the *c* before *e* and *i* from the sibilant sound of *s;* and the many Mexicanismos and words of Nahuatl origin (Entwistle 1936; Semeleder in Henríquez Ureña 1938). From the standpoint of our study, however, the most interesting features of the Spanish of Mexico City are those which serve to distinguish it from the northern Sonoran dialect and the southern Arizona dialect. Perhaps the most obvious of these is the fact that the standard intonation patterns or *sonsonete* of the Mexico City Spanish differ from the "rustic" patterns of Sonora that some of the writer's informants have described as "clipped." From the standpoint of vocabulary, the Spanish of the central area contains relatively few archaisms, and has been influenced more by the classical forms introduced into Spain in the seventeenth and eighteenth centuries. Cuervo (1935: 69) notes that in early times there was not the great distance between the "cultured" and popular language that later developed under the influence of classical studies; he adds that in books written at the time of the Conquest there appear many forms still heard among the common folk of Colombia and other Latin American countries. In contrast to southern Arizona Spanish, also, there is a much more strict use of formal Spanish between individuals who are not on intimate terms with each other. For a clerk in Mexico City to use familiar

Spanish to a customer, for example, would be grossly insulting.

Pachuco, a third variant of Spanish spoken in Tucson, might almost be described as a separate language, since it is hardly more intelligible to Spanish-speaking than it is to English-speaking people (Barker 1950). The speakers of Pachuco are very largely adolescent and young adults of Mexican descent who move in lower-class social circles. Since, in Tucson, most lower-class Mexicans live on the west side of town, the Pachuco speech community may be defined in terms of geography as well as of age and social class. Many adults of Mexican descent living on the east side of town have little or no knowledge of Pachuco. A middle-class woman of Mexican descent who teaches Spanish in the high school told the writer that prior to his investigation she had never known that there was a Pachuco dialect, despite the fact that she was born in Arizona and was thoroughly familiar with the pochismos and other expressions characteristic of southern Arizona Spanish. Similarly, the Mexican-American clerk of the County Probation Office told the writer that, accustomed as she was to dealing with other Spanish-speaking people in Tucson, she found it next to impossible to understand the speech of Pachuco gang members.

As an argot of youth, Pachuco borrows heavily not only from Mexican but from American slang.

It is perhaps this latter element of its vocabulary which makes it so difficult for Mexican speakers to understand. Words like "chante" (shanty) and "flicas" (flickers; movies) reflect American slang origin, while "guaino" (a wine-drinking souse) and "rolante" (automobile) indicate the Hispanicization and adaptation of English words.

Other prominent characteristics of Pachuco are its use of a sonorous and pompous accent, its exclusive reliance on the informal verb forms of Spanish, and finally, its use of gesture and signs to supplement its vocabulary. Several of the most obscene terms in Pachuco are indicated by signs made with the hands of the speaker. In general, it may be said that Pachuco aims to be an exclusive language, restricted to the initiated, and that it is primarily a boys' language. Many Mexican girls understand it but few use it in conversation.

The above brief notes on dialects of Spanish spoken in Tucson represent, of course, only a small fraction of the observable differences between the specific forms of these various dialects. To present a detailed study of these different forms would be an undertaking far beyond the scope of the present exploratory project. Accordingly, emphasis necessarily will be placed on the use of different languages and dialects by individuals and groups, rather than on the use of specific forms (see Table 2).

Table 2
LANGUAGE USAGE OF FAMILIES
Number of Individuals in Each Family who Speak Certain Dialects of Spanish and English

FAMILY		SPANISH			ENGLISH		
Name	Members	S. Arizona Dialect	Sonoran	Pachuco	None	Substandard	Standard
Uno	6	6	6			6	2
Tres	7	1	7		1	1	1
Diez	6	3	6			3	1
Once	9	2	9			4	1
Doce	11	1	11			1	
Trece	6	1	6		1	1	
Catorce	8	8	8		1	8	
Quince	3	1	3			1	
Veinte	5	2	1		1	1	1
Treinta	9	2	9			2	1
Cuarenta	5	1	5		1	2	1
Cincuenta	6	1	6	1	1	1	1
Seis	6	1	1				6
Ocho	4	1	1	1		1	3
Sesenta	5		5			1	4
Dos	3	1	2				3
Cuatro	4	1	2				2
Cinco	4	1	4				4
Siete	3		3				3
Nueve	5	1	2				5

Chapter 5

INDIVIDUAL LINGUISTIC SYSTEMS AND INTERPERSONAL RELATIONS

In reviewing the material on family language usage, it was evident that within each family there were important differences in the ways that individual members used and reacted to language, and in the way these individuals reacted to the social conditions around them. For this reason, three of the initial hypotheses of this thesis, that variations in language usage could be accounted for in terms of differences in socioeconomic class, of stage of assimilation, and of social participation of family units, had to be discarded. Still remaining for consideration, however, was the question of the relation between the linguistic system of the family, or family circle, and the structure of the family — a question which will be investigated in detail in Chapter 7. In this chapter, the immediate concern will be with the question of the relation between individual linguistic systems and the interpersonal relations of these individuals, both within the Mexican community and also in relations with Anglo members of the larger Tucson community.

From the standpoint of individual linguistic systems, we may distinguish four main types of systems among the individuals in this study. Corresponding with these four types of linguistic systems are parallel differences in interpersonal relations, and in types of social experience. Briefly, then, we may describe the four linguistic and social types as follows:

Bilinguals, type 1 (usually American-born): speak southern Arizona dialect of Spanish and substandard English; favor English and avoid Spanish in conversations with Anglos. Seek mobility through Anglo contacts.

Bilinguals, type 2 (including many immigrants): speak standard Mexican Spanish and substandard English; favor Spanish in conversation with Anglos and tend to be shy about their English. Seek mobility through Mexican community, or are apathetic.

Bilinguals, type 3 (mostly children of types 1 and 2): speak southern Arizona dialect of Spanish, Pachuco, and substandard English; favor special language. Reject both Mexican and Anglo groups and seek to form a society of their own.

Bilinguals, type 4 (including many "Old Families"): speak standard Spanish, southern Arizona dialect, and standard English; favor both standard English and standard Spanish. Marginal to both Mexican and Anglo groups.

With this classification in mind, let us now turn to a detailed consideration of representative individuals of each type. Starting with type 1, we find that all members of the Uno family may be included in this category. All speak the southern Arizona dialect, and all also speak substandard English. Within the limits of this system, however, there are important differences in the type and quality of expression which may be correlated with differences in interpersonal relations. The linguistic systems and interpersonal relations of various members of the family may be compared in the following way:

Joe Uno, Sr.: *Linguistic System:* Spanish further from standard than wife's. He incorporates many Pachuco and slang Mexican terms. English also further from standard than wife's. His English syntax is much influenced by Spanish, for example, he says, "You're gonna see" for "You will see." In talking to Anglo women he is very deferential and uses the form "Yes, ma'am."

Interpersonal relations: Joe comes of a family whose socioeconomic status seems to have been slightly lower than that of his wife. He has spent most of his working time in construction gangs, first as an unskilled worker and then as a skilled laborer. His main social contacts are with his own extended family and with his wife's extended family; however, as a skilled workman and subcontractor, he does have some business and social contact with middle- and upper-class Anglos and their wives.

Mrs. Uno: *Linguistic system:* Spanish shows influence of high school education. She is conscious of prestige value of good Spanish. English is substandard but very clear, fluent, and idiomatic. Vocabulary is large. She is conscious of her excellent command of English, and in mixed Anglo-Mexican conversations occasionally translates Anglo questions into Spanish for the benefit of her husband. On such occasions, however, he always answers in English.

Interpersonal relations: Mrs. Uno comes of a family of lower-middle-class status, and for many years lived on the east side of town. She has long associated with Anglos as a semiprofessional clerk and has developed a high degree of self-confidence.

María Uno: *Linguistic system:* Spanish like mother's; tries to speak standard English but is shy and self-conscious about her speech.

Interpersonal relations: María is her grandfather's favorite, and is a *madrecita* (little mother) to the other children in the Uno family. She is a strong character at home, and likes to play with younger brother and sister. She is not at all prominent at school and does not like to recite in class. As yet does not go with boys.

Dolores Uno: *Linguistic system:* Spanish like other children in the neighborhood. Refuses to speak Spanish to writer. Speaks fluent substandard English with large vocabulary for age. She is completely at ease with Anglos, although her speech has a strong Sonoran accent.

Interpersonal relations: School marks not high, except in games, in which she is a leader. Has many friends at school and in the neighborhood. Very friendly with Anglos.

Joe Uno, Jr.: *Linguistic system:* Spanish like father's but uses fewer Pachuco words. Speaks fluent substandard English with strong Sonoran accent. Vocabulary fair, but, unlike little sister, lapses into Spanish in conversing with writer.

Interpersonal relations: Plays mostly with brother and sisters, and sometimes with an older boy, José Once. Likes Anglo boys and plays with them whenever possible. Does not like Mexican-American boys of own age in neighborhood; he is afraid of them. Also is afraid of some of the girls in the neighborhood; he prefers imaginative play, with himself in adult roles, to active games with his own age-mates. His work at school is only fair. He loves to work on construction jobs as his father's assistant.

Simón Uno: *Linguistic system:* His Spanish is like that of other neighborhood children and he speaks fluently. Has a working vocabulary in English but does not make complete sentences. Has picked up many slang expressions in both Spanish and English.

Interpersonal relations: Popular and happy with children of own age in neighborhood. Also likes to play with older brother and sister, but sometimes cannot follow the rules. Wants to go to school. Is very shy with Anglo women but likes to talk to Anglo men.

As a good example of type 2 we may cite the members of the Treinta family. Mr. and Mrs. Treinta speak substandard English but can also swing into the southern Arizona dialect in talking with customers. Like their parents, the Treinta children also speak standard Mexican Spanish at home, but sometimes use a mixture of southern Arizona dialect and English in informal conversation with friends. Beyond this general similarity, which stems from the parents' immigrant background, we again find important differences which, as in the cases of the individuals already described, may be correlated with differences in interpersonal relations.

Mr. Treinta: *Linguistic system:* Speaks standard Mexican Spanish and has a vocabulary rich in Mexican slang terms and expressions. Speaks substandard English with a strong Mexican accent; enjoys speaking Spanish with Anglo friends. Takes a keen interest in seeing that his children use the "right" Spanish words.

Interpersonal relations: Maintains contact with Mexicans in Mexico and visits parents annually. He is prominent in the social life of the Tucson Mexican colony, though not at top. Is very fond of sports, especially baseball. Has some Anglo contacts through his business, but few Anglo social contacts.

Mrs. Treinta: *Linguistic system:* Speaks standard Mexican Spanish. She is very careful in her choice of expressions and reprimands her husband for his use of provincialisms. Her English is fluent but substandard.

Interpersonal relations: Has circle of friends in Mexican colony and has business relations with many Mexican housewives in the district.

Catalina Treinta: *Linguistic system:* Standard Spanish with vocabulary almost as good as parents'. English much closer to standard than parents. Avoids southern Arizona dialect of Spanish and tries to avoid mixing Spanish and English in the same conversation, but says she is not as successful at this as she was before her family moved to Tucson.

Interpersonal relations: Prominent in younger social circles of the Mexican colony. Sings Mexican songs on patriotic occasions. Has graduated from high school and business college and is now helping parents in store. Acts as father's secretary, and writes all his correspondence.

Juan Treinta: *Linguistic system:* Standard Spanish with vocabulary close to Catalina's in excellence. A good command of Mexican slang and expressions; avoids pochismos and has contempt for people who use them. English close to standard.

Interpersonal relations: Prominent in high school and in the Mexican community as a folk dancer. Assists parents in store.

Miguel Treinta: *Linguistic system:* Standard Spanish at home, but mixes English and southern Arizona dialect in conversations with age-mates. Has excellent command of American slang; avoids speaking Spanish with writer.

Interpersonal relations: Participates in junior high school student body government. Active in sports; very fond of baseball. Assists parents in store.

The Once family may be said to have the same general type of background as the Treinta family, but here again, the members show interesting variations in both linguistic behavior and interpersonal relations.

José Once, Sr.: *Linguistic system:* Standard Mexican Spanish, with very few pochismos. Very little substandard English. He always converses with the writer in Spanish, but apparently is apathetic regarding the type of Spanish spoken by his children.

Interpersonal relations: Maintains contact with Mexico, but does not mix with the Tucson Mexican colony. He participates very little in the affairs of the Mexican community outside of his own small business. Has little or no contact with Anglos. Works with other Mexicans in the Southern Pacific shops.

Mrs. Once: *Linguistic system:* Sonoran dialect of Spanish; substandard English.

Interpersonal relations: Maintains contact with Mexico through regular trips to Nogales and to visit family in Sonora.

Alicia Once: *Linguistic system:* Southern Arizona dialect; substandard English. Uses many pochismos and some Pachuco words.

Interpersonal relations: Very popular with teenage group. Attends high school and helps in father's store.

José Once, Jr.: *Linguistic system:* Speaks southern Arizona dialect and substandard English. Uses many pochismos and slang Mexican expressions.

Interpersonal relations: Attends junior high school. Helps parents in store, and makes frequent trips with mother to Sonora to get supplies.

The third main linguistic type may be exemplified by individuals such as Hernando Cincuenta, who speaks substandard English, the southern Arizona dialect, and Pachuco.

Hernando Cincuenta: *Linguistic system:* Southern Arizona dialect, substandard English, Pachuco, and American slang.

Interpersonal relations: Reared in the home of his grandfather and aunt, he has participated successively in neighborhood groups, the U.S. Army, and Southern Pacific shops. Has a large circle of friends of his own age. He works only when he needs cash, and spends much of his spare time fixing up his car, a 1939 Chevrolet.

The fourth main type may be exemplified by the heads of the Nueve family. Here the language of the parents is standard Mexican Spanish and standard English, but the children seem to have learned more standard Spanish at school than at home.

Mr. and Mrs. Nueve: *Linguistic system:* They speak standard Spanish at home but both speak English to children and grandchildren.

Interpersonal relations: Nueve is one of the leading merchants. He is active on Chamber of Commerce committees and in civic, but not social, affairs. Mrs. Nueve is the daughter of another of Tucson's "Old Families."

Luis Nueve: *Linguistic system:* Spoke southern Arizona dialect with maids in house as a child; also knows ranch Spanish. English is near standard.

Interpersonal relations: In connection with his father's business, he has come to know many ranchers and ranch hands.

Amelita Nueve: *Linguistic system:* Spoke English at home as a child and learned Spanish at college.

Interpersonal relations: Married a Spanish architect and lived for a while in Spain. Now teaches Spanish in a California high school.

An interesting variation of this type is found among the members of the Cuatro family. As in the above case, the parents speak standard Spanish and standard English, but unlike the Nueves, Mr. and Mrs. Cuatro speak to their children entirely in Spanish, while the children speak to their parents in English.

Mr. Cuatro: *Linguistic system:* Speaks standard Spanish, southern Arizona dialect, and standard English. Also has a good knowledge of American slang.

Interpersonal relations: Prominent in civic and social affairs; is officer of a leading Anglo service organization and a member of Club Latino. Has some informal relations with Anglos.

Mrs. Cuatro: *Linguistic system:* Standard Spanish and standard English. Attended the University of Arizona.

Children: *Linguistic system:* Standard English and standard Spanish. They speak only English at home and with friends. Speak both Spanish and English to relatives on both sides of the family.

Interpersonal relations: Most of their friends are Anglo children and English-speaking children of Mexican descent living on the east side of town. Mingle with Spanish-speaking Mexicans principally at gatherings of extended family.

Conclusions

Variations in the language usage are so great that the family unit cannot be used as a basis of classification for linguistic types. See, for example, the difference between the language usage of Treinta, Sr. and Miguel Treinta; also Once, Sr. and José Once, Jr. Such variations also led to the abandonment of socioeconomic class and "stage of assimilation" as possible bases for a classification of linguistic types. The variations, however, did correspond to variations in interpersonal relations and in individual social experience, and it was on this basis that the classification outlined in this chapter was established.

Chapter 6

LINGUISTIC BEHAVIOR IN THE COMMUNITY AND IN INTERPERSONAL RELATIONS

In Chapter 3, it was pointed out that the Mexican people of Tucson are more or less bicultural. Within the intimate circles of family life, Mexican cultural interests are dominant, while in their contacts with the outside world, Anglo cultural interests compete with Mexican cultural interests for their attention. More specifically, on the basis of our sociological and linguistic material, we may divide the interpersonal relations of members of the Mexican community into four main categories, or areas. These are, first, the area of intimate relations between members of the same extended family or social set; second, the area of informal relations between bilinguals of Mexican descent outside the family group; third, the area of formal relations between bilinguals; fourth, the area of relations between bilinguals and Anglos. As we have seen in our survey of cultural background, Mexican cultural interests, aided by religious influence, are dominant in the area of intimate relations while in the area of Anglo-Mexican relations the influence of Anglo urban culture competes with Mexican cultural interests for their attention. For individuals in the Mexican community, these areas may be represented as a kind of continuum, at one end of which are the intimate relations with others of Mexican descent, while at the other end are the purely formal relations with Anglos. In between are formal and informal relations with people of Mexican descent outside the family circle, and in some cases with Mexicans from Mexico.

Paralleling the above described continuum in areas of interpersonal relations is a continuum in language usage, and we find that the categories of interpersonal relations are reflected by corresponding changes in linguistic behavior. At one end of this linguistic continuum Spanish is dominant in the individuals' contacts and at the other end English is dominant. In between are the pochismos, the Pachuco dialect, and the various mixtures of the two languages. Carrying this comparison a step further, we find that the position of each family on the cultural continuum is roughly paralleled by its position on the linguistic continuum. The four groups of individuals described in Chapter 1 thus may be broadly ranged according to (1) language usage, and (2) position of the family with respect to Mexican and Anglo areas of interpersonal relations.

In their relation to these areas, the members of the first type or class described in Chapter 1 are dominated by Mexican culture in the areas of intimate relations and informal and formal relations with bilinguals. Their leaders, all of whom use standard Spanish on formal occasions, represent a small minority of the total Mexican population but are the backbone of what might be called the "Colonia Mexicana" in Tucson. The second main class may be described as dominated by Anglo culture in all areas except those of intimate relations. The third class, the Pachuco group, rejects the cultural norms of both the Anglo and Mexican groups for intimate and informal relations and substitutes those of its own, drawn from antisocial aspects of both cultures. The fourth class tries to maintain an even balance between Anglo and Mexican areas of interpersonal relations.

In the above classification the point should be stressed that in his relation to these areas, each individual is shifting constantly. The "classes" of bilingual individuals and families are highly volatile, especially for the children. The areas in which the family members operate are the basic setting for the social behavior we are studying; thus, these areas will be used as points of departure for our analysis of the relation of language usage to the life of the Mexican community and to attitudes characteristic of this minority group.

At the outset of this analysis, the point also should be made that we are dealing with individuals who speak two languages and who have the ability to use either one, at will, in any situation. Furthermore, not only the speakers but the listeners have bilingual ability in the situations in which we are interested. For it is the deliberate choice of a linguistic form in a given situation that serves to bring out the meaning of that form to its user. Most of all is this true in situations in which a speaker switches from one language to another in the course of his conversation. By analyzing the factors which cause him to do this we begin to define the functions of the two languages in the life of the minority group.

In addition to the basic premise of the bilingual ability of the speaker and hearer, then, we find that the following factors are associated with the choice of Spanish or English in any given situation:

1. Type of interpersonal relationship involved: intimate or formal, familial or economic, and so forth.

2. Subject context: what is being discussed.

3. Social context: presence or absence of Anglos or of other Mexicans, home environment, work environment, and so forth.

It is of course true that in any given conversation-event, two or more of these factors may be operating simultaneously.

The Area of Intimate Relations Among Bilinguals

Perhaps the best way to start this section of our analysis is to indicate the way in which Spanish is identified with intimate or familial relations in the Mexican community. Almost without exception, Spanish is the language of childhood and the language used by parents with children in the home. And, by extension, the informal Spanish of the home is used in informal relations with others of Mexican descent in the Tucson community. Formal Spanish is often not learned at all, and in its place, the individual uses English. The habitual speaking of Spanish to Mexicans, together with the intimacy of the linguistic forms used, makes it incongruous and almost unthinkable for some native bilinguals to use Spanish in communication with an Anglo. During the first part of the writer's stay in the El Rio district, almost all of his Mexican acquaintances addressed him in English, even though he spoke to them in Spanish. However, as he became better acquainted in the neighborhood, he received more Spanish in response to his Spanish. This was particularly apparent in his relations with the Treinta family, owners of the grocery store.

The distinction between the social functions of English and Spanish is reflected even in the imaginative play of bilingual children. Informal Spanish is usually used in make-believe games having domestic themes, while English is used in games dealing with city life, crime, military exploits, and so forth.

The formal-informal division between the use of English and Spanish may be extended even to household pets. In the Uno family, where the dog is regarded and treated largely on a casual and impersonal basis, the members constantly address him in English. On one occasion, however, when the family was getting ready to leave Tucson on a long trip and the dog had to be left behind, I heard him addressed affectionately in Spanish. In the Sesenta family, a fat black cat leads a petted and pampered existence in the household. Mrs. Sesenta, however, does not like the cat and always addresses it in English, while her daughter, who is very fond of the animal, always speaks to it in Spanish.

The Area of Formal Relations Among Bilinguals

English is used by bilinguals in the more formal types of quasi-social relations — for instance, between Boy Scout master and the troop scouts and at parents' meetings at schools. In two types of social functions in the Mexican community, however, formal Spanish, rather than English, is the language used. The first type consists of the religious services in the three Catholic churches which serve Tucson's Mexican population. Priests in all three are Spanish and speak formal Castilian in their sermons. The second type may be described as secular pro-Mexican celebrations or programs, in which Mexican-born individuals have a leading part. In formal economic relations between bilingual adults, English is frequently used, especially in situations in which the relation is of customer-employee or employer-employee type.

The Area of Informal Relations Among Bilinguals

In this area — in which most of the social life of teen-age Mexicans in Tucson takes place — a rapid shifting from one language to another is common, and often two languages may be used in the same sentence or phrase. In many such instances a shift in the subject context may be a factor in the linguistic shift, for the subject context may be so closely associated in the individual's mind with a particular language that he feels that the word or phrase "cannot be translated" into his other language.

A bilingual, however, will frequently use American slang in describing characteristically American ways of reacting to or doing things. On the other hand, in quasi-economic relations among bilinguals — for instance, between a foreman and workmen in a construction company or among clerks in a store — the informal border dialect is always used.

The Area of Anglo-Mexican Relations

While, as we have seen, Spanish is the language of intimate relations among Tucson bilinguals, there are certain occasions in which, even when talking to intimates, a bilingual may shift into English. An important factor involved in such shifts has been described as social context. Perhaps the best illustrations of this factor may be found in conversations at which Anglos are present. The fact that this shifting into English occurs even though the person of Mexican descent knows that the Anglo present can speak Spanish, suggests that Tucson Mexicans have a sense of shame or inferiority about speaking Spanish in the presence of Anglos, especially when they are uncertain as to how the Anglos regard their Mexican background. Indeed, in some instances the feeling of inferiority may be so strong that the individual may actually pretend he does not understand Spanish or may even refuse to speak it. Under conditions of emotional stress, however, a bilingual may disregard the presence of Anglos and lapse into Spanish.

While the bilingual thus often seeks to escape being labeled a Mexican, he very often fails in this objective for another reason — his English betrays a "Mexican accent." To put it more accurately, he speaks a Mexican dialect of substandard English. Not only in accent but in vocabulary, grammar, and sentence melody, his English is influenced by his Spanish. This dialect is reflected even in the written English of Mexican school children in the barrios.

What is the function of the Mexican dialect of English in Mexican-Anglo relations? It seems quite clear that it is a symbol of the inferior social status of the Mexican minority group in Tucson. The only sure way for a person of Mexican descent to avoid having this stigma placed on his child, then, is to move out of the barrios and rear his family on the east side of town. At first thought, this would not seem to be a difficult step for a Mexican whose income was large enough to make the change. The trouble is not so much financial as it is social. To move out of the barrios to the east side implies a social superiority to one's fellow residents in the barrios. It thus becomes increasingly difficult for an "east side" Mexican to maintain social relations with those in the barrios. As long as a Mexican is living in a barrio his neighbors expect him to conform to certain barrio standards of behavior. When he moves to the east side he necessarily adopts different standards. The speaking of Spanish is one of the strongest symbols of conformity to barrio life. In the presence of Anglos, as we have seen, many Mexicans prefer to speak English. But in a social setting which is dominantly Mexican, the opposite compulsion — to speak Spanish — may win out. The speaking of Spanish thus becomes a symbol of participation in a minority group. It may even be used to indicate a bond of sympathy between members of two different minorities, as between a Mexican and German prisoners-of-war who were in camps near Tucson during World War II.

Conclusions

Summarizing the above, we may say that the categories of interpersonal relations in the community, arrived at through our sociological and linguistic analyses, are paralleled by clearly defined differences in linguistic behavior in each category. In our first category, that of intimate relations, we find the intimate forms almost universally dominant. In the second category, that of informal relations between bilinguals, we find a pattern of rapid alternation between English and Spanish. In the third category, that of formal relations between bilinguals, we find English used by native Tucsonans, and formal Mexican Spanish spoken by Mexican immigrants. In the fourth category, that of Anglo-Mexican relations, we find English dominant, and Spanish avoided even though the person of Mexican descent knows that the Anglo to whom he is speaking can speak Spanish.

In the above chapter we have also seen how, in a bilingual minority group, the functions of the two languages tend to become specialized and to take on symbolic values according to the role of the group in the general community. With this picture in mind, let us now turn to a more detailed consideration of some of the important variables involved in the different ways different individuals in the minority group use and react to language.

Table 3
LANGUAGE USAGE IN PERSONAL RELATIONSHIPS

Name of Family	Parent-parent	Parent-child	Parent-relative	Child-relative	Child-child	Family-animal	Parent-Anglo	Parent-Mexican	Child-Anglo	Child-Mexican
Uno	en Sp	m Sp; so E	m Sp; so E	m Sp; so E	m Sp; so E	al en E	al en E	en Sp	m E; so Sp	m Sp; so E
Tres	en Sp	en Sp		en Sp	m Sp; so E			en Sp	en E or no E	m Sp; so E
Diez		en Sp			m Sp; so E	E-Sp	m E; so Sp	en Sp	en E	m Sp; so E
Once	en Sp	al en Sp	en Sp	en Sp	al en Sp		en Sp	en Sp	m E; so Sp	m Sp; so E
Doce	en Sp	en Sp	en Sp	en Sp	en Sp		E-Sp	en Sp	E-Sp	
Trece	en Sp	en Sp			m Sp; so E		m Sp; so E	en Sp	m Sp; so E	
Catorce		en Sp			m Sp; so E		en Sp	en Sp	m Sp; so E	m Sp; so E
Quince	en Sp	m Sp; so E	en Sp	en Sp			m E; so Sp	en Sp	en E	
Veinte	m E; so Sp	en E	E-Sp				en E	en Sp		en Sp
Treinta	en Sp	m Sp; so E			m Sp; so E	E-Sp	E-Sp	en Sp	m E; so Sp	m Sp; so E
Cuarenta		en Sp	en Sp	en Sp	en Sp		E-Sp	en Sp	en E	m Sp; so E
Cincuenta		en Sp	E-Sp	m Sp; so E	m Sp; so E		en E	en E	en E or no E	en Sp
Seis	en E	m E; so Sp	m E; so Sp	m E; so Sp	en E	en E	en E	m Sp; so E	E-Sp	E-Sp
Ocho	E-Sp	m E; so Sp	m Sp; so E	m Sp; so E	m E; so Sp	E-Sp	m E; so Sp	en Sp	en E	
Sesenta		E-Sp	m Sp; so E	m Sp; so E	en E	E-Sp	m E; so Sp	en Sp	en Sp	m E; so Sp
Dos	m Sp; so E	m E; so Sp	m Sp; so E	E-Sp		E-Sp	en E		en E	
Cuatro	en Sp	E-Sp	E-Sp	m Sp; so E	en E	en Sp	E-Sp	E-Sp	en E	
Cinco	E-Sp	m E; so Sp	m Sp; so E	m Sp; so E	m E; so Sp		en E	m Sp; so E	en E	
Siete	m E; so Sp	m Sp; so E	en Sp	en Sp		en Sp	en E	m Sp; so E	en E	en Sp
Nueve	en Sp	m E; so Sp	E-Sp	m E; so Sp	en E		en E	m Sp; so E	en E	

Abbreviations
al — almost
E — English
en — entirely
E-Sp — half English — half Spanish
m — mainly
so — some
Sp — Spanish

Chapter 7

LANGUAGE USAGE AND FAMILY STRUCTURE

Among the Mexican families in this study, the language usage within the family seems to be influenced by two aspects of family structure. The first and more obvious of these is the ethnic generation of the parents. If they are of the first or immigrant generation, their usage of and attitude toward language are likely to differ considerably from those of parents born in the United States. For the adult immigrant, Spanish is the language of his homeland. English, as his second language, is associated with his immigrant status as a member of a minority group. To the native-born American of Mexican descent, this situation is in part reversed. English, the language he uses in school, and in all subsequent relations with Anglos, links him to American life, while Spanish is indelibly associated in his mind with his family background and affiliation with a minority group.

Perhaps because of these differences in linguistic and social experience, immigrants and native-born parents have different ways of regarding the linguistic development of their children. Native-born parents seem to take the speaking of the southern Arizona dialect in the family circle as a matter of course. For immigrant parents, however, the decision is not so simple. An immigrant couple starting to rear a family in a Mexican neighborhood in Tucson would seem to have three main alternatives open to them. These alternatives are: (1) to teach the children to speak the parents' own variant of Mexican Spanish; (2) to be apathetic with respect to the type of Spanish spoken by the children; and (3) to discourage the speaking of Spanish among the children.

While our data are too limited to draw definite conclusions on this point, it may be suggested that immigrant parents tend to select the alternative which is most consistent with their own social goals. If they desire to move in upper-class Mexican circles, either in Tucson or in Mexico, they will try to teach their children "good Spanish." If they are content to move in lower-class or lower-middle-class circles in the Tucson Mexican community, their attitude toward their children's Spanish will tend to be apathetic. If they are interested in raising their status in the Anglo community, immigrant parents may actually discourage their children from speaking Spanish.

The Treinta family would seem to provide a good illustration of the first alternative. Mr. and Mrs. Treinta, as we have seen, speak standard Mexican Spanish. Although they live in a neighborhood in which almost everyone speaks the southern Arizona dialect, they have reared their children to speak standard Mexican Spanish at home. Both they and their children tend to look down on the use of pochismos as a mark of inferior social status. Finally, both parents seek and find prestige as prominent members of Tucson's Mexican community.

As an example of the second alternative, which seems to be the one most frequently chosen by immigrants in Tucson barrios, we may take the case of the Once family. While Once still speaks standard Mexican Spanish and his wife speaks the Sonoran dialect of Spanish, the children speak entirely in the southern Arizona dialect and use many pochismos. In the course of the years, the influence of the children's Spanish actually has outweighed that of the parents, so that, according to Alicia Once, her father's Spanish is taking on the attributes of the southern Arizona dialect. The difference in the usage of the two families, Treinta and Once, may be correlated not only with different social goals but with the different fields of interpersonal relations in which the members operate.

The Veinte family provides a clear illustration of the third alternative. Francisco Veinte immigrated to Tucson from Mexico as a boy, went through the Tucson school system, and had two years of college. Then he married a half-Anglo, half-Mexican girl and they settled in the new neighborhood of El Rio. Francisco and his wife speak English to each other and to their child, but have been unable to get their little girl to break away from conformity to the Spanish usage of other children in the neighborhood.

In regard to the usage of English, it is interestng to note that in all of the immigrant families in his study having school-age children, there is evidence of some use of English among the children in the home. This evidence is in line with the data from our questionnaires which indicate that the English usage among children in families in which one or more parents are of the immigrant generation actually is greater than that among children of native-born parents who live in a Mexican neighborhood. The explanation of this unexpected situation may be in part ascribed to the fact that children of immigrants are sensitive to the immigrant status of their parents, and are anxious to avoid the stigma of the immigrant group by overcoming the linguistic handicap. Even more important, however, is the point that the children of immigrants are relatively free from family pressure, a point which we shall now take up as the second main aspect of family structure which has relevance to this study.

By family pressure is meant the influence of the extended family on the life of any given family unit. Among the native-born families of Mexican descent in Tucson, this pressure is heavy, since families are very large and many families have lived and intermarried with other Mexican families in Tucson for several generations. To take the Uno family, for example, Mrs. Uno has over twenty nephews and nieces on her side of the family alone, and this does not include numerous ceremonial relationships of godparent, godchild, and the like. Since almost all of these relatives live in Tucson, and since they see each other and visit in each other's houses at regular intervals, there is very little that goes on within any given family unit that escapes discussion in the extended family. But even more important, the standards of behavior for the various family units are set by the heads of the older generation. This means that divergencies from the traditional way of doing things are sure to be reported to the grandparental generation, with resulting displeasure and sorrow on the part of all concerned. The speaking of Spanish within the family is, of course, one of the most deep-rooted among all these traditions, and it follows that the extended family tends to preserve its use.

When, as often occurs, members of three or more generations live together under the same roof, the influence of the extended family is even more direct. The Cincuenta household is a good example. "Grandpa" Cincuenta, his daughter Alicia, his grandson Hernando, and Mr. and Mrs. Cincuenta, Jr., all speak fluent English, but when the writer asked what language the family used to talk with three-year-old Andrés Cincuenta, "Grandpa" replied, "Oh, Spanish!" A similar situation exists in the Cuarenta household. Here the youngest grandchild, little Carolina, is spoken with in Spanish by everyone, even by the high-school-age girl, Beatriz.

Interesting variation in the pattern of family language usage may be seen in instances in which family units have been able to break away from the influence of the extended family. We have already mentioned the case of the Veinte family. The Dos family seems to have relieved family pressure by moving to an apartment in an Anglo neighborhood. Mr. and Mrs. Dos still speak Spanish to each other but they converse with their little girl entirely in English. Dos says the child refuses to speak Spanish, although she understands it.

In the Cuatro family, also on the east side, a similar situation prevails, but here the influence of the extended family is so important, and the family itself is so prominent in Mexican affairs, that the Cuatro children have to make concessions to their ancestral tongue. As in the Dos family, Mr. and Mrs. Cuatro speak to each other in Spanish, but they also speak to the children in Spanish, while the latter reply to their parents in English. The children, in turn, have to speak some Spanish with the members of the older generation on both sides of the family.

In the Cinco family, the parents' position is delicate, owing to the fact that not only are both members of prominent Mexican families, but Cinco is prominent as a public official as well. Hence the effort in the family is to strike an even balance between the two languages. Mr. and Mrs. Cinco apparently speak to each other and to their children about half in English and half in Spanish. The children, however, speak to each other and to their parents mainly in English. Grandparents on both sides of the family speak to the children in Spanish. The children customarily address Cinco's parents in English, but to Mrs. Cinco's parents, who live on the west side of town, they always speak Spanish.

In the Siete family, the only child, a boy of four, is the subject of much linguistic experimentation on the part of his elders. Since the child's parents have separated, the child has come under the influence of his maternal grandparents and great-grandparents who speak to him entirely in

Spanish. The child's mother, fearing that he would forget his English, now makes it a rule to speak to him in English. The child speaks English to his playmates in an Anglo neighborhood and his Spanish shows some English influence. Because of this, his great-grandfather teases the child and calls him a "Pochi."

Conclusions

Two aspects of family structure affect the linguistic behavior of any given family, namely the ethnic generation of the parents, and the pressure of the extended family.

The social functions of the ancestral language differ according to the immigrant or native-born generation of the parents. For immigrants, the language of childhood and the one with which they are most familiar, is standard Mexican Spanish or a variant thereof. In moving into a Tucson Mexican neighborhood, therefore, immigrants find themselves facing three alternatives: (1) to teach their child Mexican Spanish; (2) to be apathetic and allow the child to speak the southern Arizona dialect; and (3) to actively discourage Spanish. Our linguistic evidence suggests that the immigrant parents select the alternative which is most consistent with their social goals. For native-born parents, as well as for the children of immigrants, the southern Arizona dialect becomes identified with the minority group. As such, its widest use is in the Pochi family circle.

Pressure of the extended family induces conformity to the behavior patterns of the older generation. Family pressure varies directly with the proximity of family units to each other. Because of this fact, native-born families usually are subject to greater pressure than are immigrant families if such native-born families live on the west side of town.

Chapter 8

LANGUAGE USAGE AND THE NEIGHBORHOOD

It has been pointed out previously that Tucson's barrios are distinct geographic units, each of which has a very high percentage of Mexican-American residents. Taken together, they comprise what we may describe as the Mexican neighborhood in Tucson. This neighborhood is to be distinguished from the Mexican community, of which it is a part. For, as has been pointed out, some members of the Mexican community live outside the barrios on the west side of town. The membership of these people in the Mexican community can be detected only through personal traits and through their social participation. This means that the chief visible aspect of the Mexican community is the neighborhood. For this reason, Mexicans and Anglos alike have come to identify the neighborhood as a symbol of the Mexican community. Persons of Mexican descent who live in this neighborhood are expected to conform to Mexican standards of behavior. There is only one way to escape such conformity with impunity. This is to move out of the neighborhood.

The language of the neighborhood is, of course, Spanish. Here again, the southern Arizona dialect has come to symbolize the Tucson Mexican community. Anyone who speaks the language of the *calle* is considered a neighbor. Those who refuse to speak Spanish are regarded as snobs or outsiders. In this connection, it should be emphasized that the speaking of the southern Arizona dialect is not limited to the lower-class Mexican neighborhoods on the west side of town. Many bilinguals of middle- and upper-class status in the Mexican community also use many of its forms. Many upper-class bilinguals actually speak less standard Mexican Spanish than middle- and lower-class immigrants, as is attested by statements on the language usage of members of the Club Latino and Club Anahuac. The main difference in the Spanish usage of native bilinguals living outside the neighborhood seems to be that, by reason of education and other social experience, some of them are more conscious than native-born barrio residents of the "errors" of the southern Arizona dialect. These east-side bilinguals seek to substitute standard Spanish forms in all conversation with cultivated Spanish-speaking persons from other countries. If they wish to maintain their connections in the barrios, however, they make use of the southern Arizona dialect. Thus Mr. Treinta uses some of its expressions in waiting on customers at his store; a Padre uses it in giving catechismal instructions to El Rio children; Mr. Tres uses it in speaking to old friends; and Mr. Cinco uses it in talking informally with the parents of the children who attend his school.

While people who are marginal to the Mexican community may speak the southern Arizona dialect only on certain occasions, those who live in the neighborhood speak it a large part of the time. This is true not only of the women and children, who spend most of their time in the neighborhood, but also of the men, most of whom are out of it during the day. The explanation is that as members of the same occupational group these men can only obtain jobs in fields open to other Mexicans, and accordingly continue to speak Spanish to their neighbors on the job.

This brings us to the point that conformity to neighborhood standards is not only culture-typed to the pattern of the Mexican community, but is also class-typed, since a very large proportion of the neighborhood is lower class, from the standpoint of both the Anglo and Mexican communities. Evidence of this two-dimensional conformity may be seen in almost every household, in the correlation of traits of Mexican material culture with traits which may be described as lower class in the general Tucson community, such as house type, yard, plumbing, furniture, style of dress, and type of vehicle owned.

From this evidence it may be seen that the language of the neighborhood is part of a pattern of conformity to neighborhood class and cultural norms. To understand how this pattern of conformity is achieved, it is necessary to examine briefly the social structure of the neighborhood. In the first place, we may note that in such an ethnic minority neighborhood people seem to be in closer relations to one another than in many Anglo neighborhoods. The basis for this seems to be both socioeconomic and cultural. In the Mexican neighborhood, houses are closer together, families are larger, and there is less privacy. While this does not mean that neighbors will become acquainted, it does enable them to observe each other's behavior with greater ease than in Anglo middle- or upper-class neighborhoods. Added to this, there is, in the Mexican neighborhood as we have seen, a network of familial relationships which makes the behavior of the individual family unit even more conspicuous.

Outside the immediate pressure of close neighbors and relatives, barrio residents are influenced to conform by a group of institutions which center in the neighborhood. Foremost among these is the Catholic Church which reaches 90 percent of the families of Mexican descent through its parish organization. At Santa Margarita Chapel, which serves the El Rio district, the priest gives all his sermons and announcements in Spanish. In addition, all of the meetings of parish organizations, such as women's groups, young peoples' groups, and the like, are conducted in Spanish. The *doctrina,* or catechism, class does have an English section, but the enrollment totals only 10 percent of the more than one hundred pupils in regular attendance.

Another neighborhood institution which tends to foster the speaking of Spanish is, strangely enough, the playground of the American public school. Inside the school buildings children are required to speak English, but outside there are no restrictions, and schools which once tried to require English on the playground have given up. Once outside the formal atmosphere of the classroom, Mexican-American pupils seem to have an almost irresistible impulse to revert to the informal southern Arizona dialect at play. The one factor that might prevent this reversion — the presence of a large number of pupils of other ethnic groups — is missing, since there are few, if any, non-Mexicans living in the Mexican neighborhood. The use of Spanish in informal games is carried over to informal relations generally on the playground. At lunch time the use of Spanish is encouraged in the lunch stands just across the street from the school yard, where children may go to get tortillas and colas, and to play Mexican records on the jukebox.

The neighborhood business establishments may, in general, be included in the class of institutions that foster the speaking of Spanish. Most of these establishments are small corner-groceries run either by families of Mexican descent or by Chinese. The Chinese have learned to speak fluent Spanish, and while they also speak good English, will almost invariably converse in Spanish with their Mexican customers. One of the largest business establishments adjoining El Rio Barrio is the dance hall known as the "Blue Moon." This is the favorite dance hall of the entire Mexican community. In addition, it is used for parties of several of the most prominent organizations in the Mexican community. On each of several visits to the hall, the writer noted that while English was occasionally used in formal introductions, the main language of people in the hall was Spanish. Also, all announcements at these Mexican-American affairs were in Spanish. On the one exception to this statement known to the writer, the master of ceremonies who spoke a phrase in English was heckled for his indiscretion, and had to repeat his remarks in Spanish.

Evidence of neighborhood influence on the language usage of family circles may be seen in the cases of new families whose membership includes individuals who prior to their arrival in the barrios spoke mainly English. Such a case is that of the family of Joe Uno's brother. Prior to moving to El Rio, this family had lived in a cosmopolitan district of Los Angeles. When they first moved into the Tucson Mexican neighborhood, the children understood Spanish but spoke very little. Within three months they were more fluent in Spanish than in English. Another illustration, already referred to in another connection, is that of the Veinte family. Mrs. Veinte, born and reared in Los Angeles, had spoken both English and Spanish at home as a child, and after their marriage she and her Mexican-born husband decided they would speak only English to their children. The influence of El Rio Barrio, however, proved too strong for little Berta, who, apparently fearing the ridicule of her playmates, became equally determined to speak to her parents and friends only in Spanish. Further evidence along this line may be seen in the instance of families in the neighborhood in which the parents are of mixed Anglo and Mexican stock. Of six cases reported to the writer in the El Rio and Barrio Libre districts, the family language in each instance continued to be Spanish. The principals of Carrillo and El Rio schools each listed four cases of Anglo-Mexican marriages; in addition, six cases of Mexican-Negro marriages were listed; in all of these Spanish was the language of the home.

When a family moves out of the Mexican neighborhood, the linguistic changes that occur may be in part attributed to freedom from family pressure, as we have seen, but they are also traceable to a release from neighborhood pressure. This may be clearly seen in the cases of families living in intermediate or "neutral" neighborhoods. While the family may continue to speak mainly Spanish at home and with relatives, there is much more opportunity in such a district for the speaking of English. In the Ocho household, for example, the two girls attend the South Side Catholic Church where services are in English, and where over half the congregation is English-speaking. Also, they attend schools in which the majority of the pupils are of Anglo descent. Further evidence on this point may be seen in a comparison of the reports of language habits of sixth-grade children of Mexican descent in the Government Heights School (in a "neutral" neighborhood) with those of children in the same grade in El Rio School.

Conclusions

As the visible symbol of the Tucson-Mexican community, the neighborhood upholds conformity to Mexican cultural traditions and to the speaking of the southern Arizona dialect, which is in turn symbolic of the neighborhood group.

A member of the Tucson Mexican community can disassociate himself from the community only by moving out of the Mexican neighborhood and by refusing to speak the southern Arizona dialect.

The linguistic and other social behavior of residents in the Mexican neighborhood is class-typed as well as culture-typed.

Conformity in linguistic and other social behavior is obtained not only through family pressure but also through the neighborhood structure — that is, through the pressure of immediate neighbors, and the pressure of neighborhood institutions.

The influence of the neighborhood on language usage varies according to the degree to which the neighborhood separates family units from outside majority group influences.

Chapter 9

LANGUAGE USAGE AND CULTURAL ORIENTATION

Among the individuals studied in this thesis, we have noted marked variations in linguistic and other social behavior, even between individuals in the same family. A detailed study of some of these instances presented in Chapter 5 led to the conclusion that differences in individual linguistic behavior are congruent with that individual's system of interpersonal relations. Further, it was indicated in Chapter 6 that such systems vary according to the individual relation to the main fields of interpersonal relations, or psychosocial fields, which characterize life in the Mexican community. Finally, a comparison of individual differences in linguistic and other social behavior, revealed that the individuals could be grouped into four main types, each of which differed from the other three in language usage and social experience.

While the above analysis has shown the correlation between linguistic and nonlinguistic behavior, it still leaves unanswered the question of how different individuals select different fields of interpersonal relations. In part, of course, this question may be explained by differences in age, sex, and social background of the various members of a family. No explanation would be complete, however, without some reference to the problem of motivation. Reexamining our material from this standpoint, we find that each of our four types of individuals also may be described in terms of the social role which they either occupy or expect to occupy in the community. Those in the first group, for example, seek mobility through Anglo contacts with the ultimate objective of becoming full-fledged members of the Anglo community. Those in the second group seek mobility through the Mexican community, if at all, and seem content to be regarded as Mexicans. Those in the third group, failing to find their goals in either the Anglo or Mexican communities, seek them outside both groups. Those in the fourth group seek goals that are highly valued by both the Anglo and Mexican groups.

With these different types of social roles in mind, let us now turn to the question of how such roles are selected. On the level of social psychology, with which we are here concerned, numerous theories have been advanced to account for apparent individual differences in motivation. Four of the most prominent of these will be referred to here, and an attempt will be made to apply them to the selection of roles by members of the Tucson Mexican community. Of special interest in connection with this survey will be the question of the place which each theory assigns to language in the process of role selection. An attempt will be made to see how orientation with respect to Mexican and Anglo cultures may affect the linguistic behavior of representative individuals in each group.

Perhaps the most widely accepted theory as to how social roles are selected is that of stimulus-response or conditioning. This theory holds that the individual's role in society is established through a learning process of trial and error which begins in childhood. Those responses of the individual that are rewarded tend to persist, while those which are not rewarded, or are punished, tend to be lost, or extinguished. With this basis, Miller and Dollard (1941: 183ff) and other investigators have set up a theory of social learning and have added the mechanism of "learning by imitation" to account for the acquisition of much learned social behavior. Learning by imitation is most likely to occur, according to these investigators, in social conditions of hierarchy or rank with regard to specific skills and social statuses. They point out that there seem to be at least four classes of persons who are imitated by others. They are: (1) superiors in an age-grade hierarchy, (2) superiors in a hierarchy of social status, (3) superiors in an intelligence ranking system, and (4) superior technicians in any field.

Another prominent theory as to how social roles are established is that of cultural patterning.

Using the premise that value systems, including goals, are created in the individual through culturally established modes of behavior, Kardiner (1945) and others have elaborated a theory of basic personality structure. This theory suggests that the character and limits of an individual's value system and goals are set in the first few years of life, through socially accepted modes of nursing, toilet training, and so forth. Variations are to be accounted for in terms of abnormality in physical characteristics or in the particular family situation.

A third theory, that of the Gestalt psychologists, differs from those described above by looking for the explanation of how social roles are established in the relation of the individual to one or more psychological fields, rather than to early environmental conditions. By psychological field is meant an area of attention or perception within which a person or object has a psychological attraction or repulsion for another individual. The goals of any given individual thus are ordered by the structure of the fields in which he participates (Brown 1936).

A fourth theory, that of the social behaviorists (Mead 1931), asserts that the social roles of any given individual are determined by the way in which that individual conceives of his role or function in his environment. According to this theory, the individual's concept of his own self arises through conduct, when he becomes a social object in experience to himself. (By "social objects" is meant "other living forms in the group to which the organism belongs" [Mead].) This takes place when the individual uses and responds to attitudes, gestures, and other symbols as would another individual in the same situation. The beginning of this distinctly human use of significant symbols occurs in childhood, largely through his assuming the roles of others in play behavior. In this unfolding conception of the self, language plays a crucial part, since it provides the chief way through which the individual can take the role of "the other" and thus further develop his concept of his own role in society.

A review of the above theories suggests the following explanation. The individuals who are members of the various family units are of different ages and differ from each other in their contacts with the psychosocial fields operating in the community. Further, individuals differ in physical type, skin color, temperament, linguistic system, and many other personal characteristics. These differences, many of which have become fixed early in life, affect the ways in which the particular individual and those around him conceive of his social role. This conception, in turn, will influence the type of social contacts he will seek and the type of individual he will select as models for his own goals and values in the general community.

The theories we have discussed have in common the point that different individuals are affected by different aspects of the social environment, and that these differences in social experience give rise to differences in motivation. This generalization suggests the following statement as an operating hypothesis: Differences in linguistic and social behavior between individuals in the same family may be correlated with differences in cultural orientation. This orientation will vary according to the goals which, by means of his social experience, any given individual finds accessible to him.

To test this hypothesis, let us now examine some of the cases in this study of individual differences within family units. In the Treinta family interesting differences may be noted in the linguistic and other social behavior of father and sons. Linguistically, the main difference is in the command of English. Mr. Treinta speaks English with a marked accent and with substandard grammar. Both his sons speak much nearer standard English, and the younger boy, Miguel, is adept at American slang. The older boy, Juan, seems to have a better command of Mexican Spanish, however, and like his father, has a rich vocabulary of Mexican slang. Father and sons also differ in their willingness to speak Spanish with Anglos. Mr. Treinta never misses an opportunity to do so, while the boys, especially Miguel, are reticent. In interpersonal relations, the father is prominent in the group of Mexican-born businessmen known as the Club Anahuac and his wife is a leader in the Mexican community's social affairs. As we have already seen, the family has gained prominence in the Mexican community through the participation of the children in patriotic programs, community dances, and recitals. In regard to relations with Anglos, Mr. and Mrs. Treinta's contacts are mainly through their store. Both boys, however, are prominent at school, and Miguel is president of the junior high school student body.

Mr. and Mrs. Treinta are strongly oriented toward Mexico. The parents and relatives of both are there, and both feel that Mexico is their home. However, they are reconciled to the fact that the boys feel quite differently. Mr. Treinta told the writer that while he and his wife feel that Mexico is their home, the boys prefer to live in the United States. His chief interest in his store, therefore, is for his sons. The boys themselves have their goals in the United States, but are not so sure that they want to stay in their father's business. Juan has expressed an interest in becoming a pharmacist, while Miguel thinks he wants to be a lawyer. The boys tend to select Anglo fields of interpersonal relations to advance as "Spanish-Americans" in the Anglo community, while their parents, as Mexicans, must be content with securing their prestige in Mexico and in Tucson's "Colonia Mexicana."

Summarizing this case, we note that individual differences in age-grade and social experience are accompanied by corresponding differences in social goals and in cultural orientation.

In the Once family, we may note marked differences in the linguistic and other social behavior of José Once, Sr., and his children, especially Alicia, and José, Jr. Once, Sr., it will be recalled, speaks Mexican Spanish and broken English, and works as a skilled laborer. Outside of his work, he participates very little in either the Mexican or Anglo community, and on the basis of his own statements his attitude may be described as apathetic. His orientation is toward Mexico, and it is his contact with Mexicans in Mexico that is his chief source of social prestige. His children, on the other hand, find that they are not socially accepted either among Anglos in the United States or among Mexicans in Mexico, and accordingly find their goals limited to those of the Tucson Mexican community, or failing this, in the still more segregated Pachuco group.

In the Veinte family, both Mr. and Mrs. Veinte recognize that their hope of mobility lies in disassociating themselves from the Mexican community and identifying themselves as "Spanish-Americans" in the Anglo community. Their small daughter acts on a different basis, however, since her goals are the immediate ones of recognition and approval among the Spanish-speaking children in the Mexican neighborhood where the family lives. Her parents can see that as the child grows older she may obtain quite different goals, provided she can pass as a Spanish-American, but the child herself cannot yet see this. In this case, again, we note that individual differences in age-grade and social experience are accompanied by corresponding differences in the goals selected.

Conclusions

The above evidence would seem to support the hypothesis that there is a positive relation between social goals, cultural orientation, and individual linguistic behavior, and the fields of interpersonal relations in which the individual participates. As a means of understanding the role of linguistic behavior in this relation, it is suggested that acceptance in any given field of interpersonal relations depends to a large degree on the ability of the individual to master the idiom of that field. This is perhaps one of the principal reasons why immigrants such as Mr. Treinta, Mr. Once, and Mr. Trece do not seek mobility for themselves in the Anglo community. Their Mexican accents are too strong to allow them to enter freely into upper-class Anglo circles, even if they should be able to achieve the other status marks of "Spanish-Americans." This situation also explains the anxiety of Mr. Cuatro, Mr. Veinte, and others to have their children speak good English so that they will not feel the social stigma of "Mexican" status.

Chapter 10

RESUME AND CONCLUSIONS

The conclusions of this study fall into three general categories: first, those relating to the problems of how language functions in a bilingual minority group in process of cultural change; second, those relating to what the linguistic behavior of individuals and groups reveals as to the conditions of acculturation and assimilation prevailing in the area studied; and, third, those relating to the value of the types of linguistic data used as a method of social research. An attempt will now be made to summarize the conclusions in each category and to review briefly the manner in which these conclusions were reached.

In order to discover how language functions in a bilingual minority group in process of cultural change, we have examined, first, the language usage and interpersonal relations of individuals who are members of representative families in the bilingual community of Tucson, Arizona; second, the usage of bilingual social groups in the community; and, third, the linguistic and cultural contacts between bilinguals and members of the larger Tucson community. We have drawn our data from three sources: first, observational studies of individuals and families; second, observation of group activities; and, third, observation of, supplemented by questionnaires on, the cultural interests of Mexican children and their families. In the course of assembling this material we have formulated and tested a series of hypotheses on the problem. The hypothesis which in the final stage of the inquiry was considered most plausible is the following:

In a bilingual minority group in process of cultural change the functions originally performed by the ancestral language are divided between two or more languages, with the result that each language comes to be identified with certain specific fields of interpersonal relations. Thus for each individual, language takes on symbolic values which vary according to the individual's social experience. The character of this experience, in turn, depends on, first, the position of the minority group in the general community; second, the relation of the individual to the bilingual group; and, third, the relation of the individual to the general community.

Corollaries:

1. The individual's pattern of linguistic behavior is congruent with his system of interpersonal relations.
2. The group's pattern of linguistic behavior is congruent with its system of interpersonal relations.
3. The linguistic systems of the bilingual individual and group may be used as indices to the conditions of assimilation and acculturation in the area studied.

Since a careful check of the above evidence has failed to produce negative cases, and since the hypothesis seems to provide a satisfactory explanation for the wide variations in linguistic behavior among the bilingual individuals involved, our conclusion is that this hypothesis may be accepted in preference to the only alternative known to be remaining — an explanation in terms of chance. Conclusions as to the various parts of the hypothesis may be summarized as follows:

The first proposition, that in a bilingual minority group in process of cultural change the functions originally performed by the ancestral language are divided between two or more languages, with the result that each language comes to be identified with certain specific fields of interpersonal relations, is supported by the evidence. The study indicated, in this regard, that Spanish came to be identified in the Mexican community as the language of intimate and family relations, while English came to be identified as the language of formal social relations and of all relations with Anglos. The study further indicated that in the social field of informal relations between bilinguals, a mixture of Spanish and English or rapid alternation between the two is common usage. Formal Spanish is used only by those Mexicans whose social relations include relations with Mexicans from Mexico.

The second proposition, that for each individual, each language used takes on a symbolic value depending on the position of the ethnic group and the relation of the individual to the group and to the general community, is supported by the evidence. We have seen how, on the basis of their use of and reaction to language, the individuals in this study may be divided into four groups, each of which corresponds to a different social relation to the ethnic and dominant communities. People seeking mobility in the Anglo community tend to avoid the southern Arizona dialect in the presence of Anglos and to place a high value on speaking "good" English. People in the Mexican community who have retained their affiliation with Mexico tend to favor Spanish in their conversations with Anglos. A third group is made up of a younger American-born generation, who reject both Spanish and English in favor of their own language, Pachuco, and who correspondingly reject the conventional social standards of the Anglo and Mexican communities. The fourth group, the "Old Families," on the upper border of both the Anglo and Mexican communities, tries to maintain a precarious balance both in its social relations and its usage of standard Spanish and standard English.

The first corollary, that the individual's pattern of linguistic behavior (language usage) is congruent with his system of interpersonal relations, is supported by the evidence. In Chapter 5, we saw how even within the same family, differences in interpersonal relations were reflected in differences in the individual's linguistic system. We also saw how these differences could be correlated with differences in age-grade and ethnic generation.

The second corollary, that the group's pattern of linguistic behavior (language usage) is congruent with its interpersonal relations, is supported by the evidence. In Chapter 6, we saw how each of the four main categories of linguistic behavior is paralleled by an equivalent category of interpersonal relations. In the category or field of intimate and familiar relations members of the Mexican community speak Spanish. In the category of informal relations with bilinguals they speak a mixture of Spanish and English. In the category of formal relations with bilinguals they speak either English or standard Mexican Spanish. In the category of relations with Anglos they speak entirely English and deliberately avoid Spanish. Finally, in Chapters 7 and 8, we have seen how the linguistic behavior patterns of the family circle and neighborhood reflect aspects of family structure and neighborhood social organization.

The third corollary, that the linguistic behavior systems of the bilingual individual and group may be used as indices of the conditions of assimilation and acculturation, is supported by the evidence. In Chapters 5 and following we have seen how different aspects of our linguistic data reflect the following acculturation and assimilation conditions in the Tucson area:

1. Psychological, as well as social subordination of the Mexican population in the general Tucson community, as indicated by
   a) reticence of Mexicans to speak Spanish with, and in the presence of, Anglos;
   b) identification of the term "Mexican" with lower-class status in Tucson, and corresponding substitution of the term "Spanish-American" for Mexicans having upper-class status;
   c) lack of informal interpersonal relations between Anglos and Mexicans as indicated by lack of informal linguistic categories common to both. Very few Mexicans can "kid" and use small-talk entirely in English in a manner common among Anglos. Also, very few Anglos can speak the mixed Spanish-English common in informal usage among Tucson Mexicans.

2. Cultural, as well as physical, segregation of the Mexican population in the general Tucson community, as indicated by
   a) inability of many young Mexicans to free themselves of a "Spanish accent" in speaking English;
   b) inability of many young Mexicans to translate Spanish expressions into English expressions;
   c) complete dependence on Spanish in certain fields of interpersonal relations.

3. Competition of U.S. and Mexican culture at various social levels in the Tucson Mexican community, as indicated by the development and function of pochismos and other hybrid forms.

4. Divergent types of cultural orientation, and correspondingly divergent social goals, in the Tucson Mexican population, as indicated by variations in language usage.

The conclusions reached as to the validity of the third corollary above may be said to constitute the conclusions of the second general category described above.

This brings us to the third main category, relating to the value of the type of linguistic data used as a method of social research. The critical question here would seem to be, "What advantages does this method offer as contrasted to existing sociological methods of solving the same type of problem?" To answer this question it will be necessary to review briefly the concept of language usage. This concept, it will be recalled, rests on the postulate that the linguistic behavior of any given individual exhibits a systematic patterning which can be defined objectively in terms, first, of the limits of the system; second, of the parts of which it is composed; and, third, of the relative frequency of use of the various parts in standard situations. Thus language usage is concerned not so much with what an individual says his attitudes and values are (i.e., how he rationalizes) as with how he uses and reacts to the linguistic symbol systems at his command in the course of his daily contacts. An Anglo resident of Tucson may say he is "very fond of the Mexican people," but such a statement cannot be given much weight in comparison with data on his language usage which shows that in his social and economic relations he clearly places Mexicans in a subordinate role, while he refers to those who are his social equals not as Mexicans but as "Span-ish-Americans" or members of "Old Families." The method of language usage, then, would seem to have an advantage over direct questions obtained through formal interviews and questionnaires, which too often are rationalizations of what the subject considers his attitudes are supposed to be.

A second principal advantage of the method of language usage would seem to lie in the fact that it offers a means of obtaining an independent check on other sociological data. Since the linguistic system of an individual or group functions as an autonomous, self-contained system, this system may be analyzed and reported on independently of other cultural data. Here again, the fact that language enters intimately and almost unconsciously into the defining and constant redefining of all interpersonal relations, makes possible a relatively high degree of objectivity in the analysis of interpersonal relations from the data of language usage.

In summary, it is perhaps not too much to say that the study of language usage may provide the basis for a new and widely applicable method of sociological analysis. The problem of the further development of this method, together with its possible applications, will be described in the following chapter.

Chapter 11

SUGGESTIONS FOR FURTHER RESEARCH

Further research in the field of social functions of language may be expected to follow along two main lines: first, the development of language usage as a more precise tool of sociological analysis, and second, the application of this tool in the study of that aspect of social behavior in which it may be most effectively used, namely, in the investigation of interpersonal relations, with special reference to attitudes. Progress along the first line will be dependent upon the more precise description and analysis of variations of linguistic behavior in social situations, and upon the statement of these relations in quantitative terms. Research along the second line may be conducted on several different levels: these range from the psychological level, on which the concern is with individual personalities, to the cultural level, on which the concern is with the language, goals, and values of larger groups of people.

The problem of quantifying data on language usage is complicated, as we have seen, by the fact that quantitative material has no sociological significance unless considered in relation to sociological situations. The problem thus involves not only the quantification of language usage but of quantifying or standardizing situations as well. The writer has no ready-made solution for this problem, but experience in field work for the present study suggests the following procedure as an approach toward quantification.

Sample Procedure — for Individuals

1. Examine sample of total linguistic behavior of individual and find limits of system (language and dialects);
2. Classify total linguistic behavior into component parts:
   a) Forms used (language, dialects, colloquial phrases, slang words, and so forth);
   b) Modes used (formal, informal, and so forth);
3. Classify types of social situations in which the individual operates (immediate family, family with outsiders, and so forth);

4. Test relative frequency of various forms and modes in standardized types of social situations, obtaining language usage of individual;
5. Evaluate language usage in terms of theory of social functions of language:
   a) Limits and categories of the individual's interpersonal relations:
      (1) Definition of group or groups to which the individual belongs, and
      (2) Status of individual in each group;
   b) Nature of the individual's interpersonal relations (attitudes) in each category.

Sample Procedure — for Groups

1. Examine sample of total linguistic behavior of group and find limits of system.
2. Classify total linguistic behavior into component parts:
   a) Forms used (language, dialects, colloquial phrases, slang words, and so forth);
   b) Modes used.
3. Classify types of situations in which members of a group operate:
   a) Meetings of entire group;
   b) Meetings of smaller groups of members;
   c) Conversations of members with outsiders.
4. Test relative frequency of various forms and modes in standardized types of social situations.
5. Evaluate language usage in terms of theory of social functions of language:
   a) Limits and categories of interpersonal relations of group members:
      (1) Definition of subgroups;
      (2) Ranking of subgroups;
      (3) Relation of group members to outsiders.
   b) Nature of interpersonal relations (attitudes) of individuals in each category.

As the above procedure indicates, the distinct advantage of this method of sociological analysis lies in the fact that the linguistic behavior of any given individual or group can be disentangled from other aspects of cultural behavior and may be studied as a self-contained system whose limits and elements may be clearly and objectively defined. In this way, as Halpern has pointed out in a letter to the author, it becomes possible to describe the social relations of an individual or group with something approaching the systematic clarity with which we can define the individual or group's linguistic behavior.

With respect to the application of language usage to the study of social behavior, prospective research again may be divided into two main aspects: first, the study of the interpersonal relations and attitudes of monolingual individuals and groups, and, second, the more specialized study of the interpersonal relations and attitudes of bilingual individuals and groups. Since the writer's thesis has been concerned with the specific problem of the Mexican-American minority, his specific suggestions for further research will be limited to that field. As has been indicated, two main types of problems may immediately be defined: first, the background study of monolingual Mexicans as potential immigrants and, second, the study of Mexican-American bilinguals.

The Study of Monolingual Mexicans as Potential Immigrants

As one approach to the analysis of a current social process, the folk background of the Mexican immigrant to the United States has been studied by Redfield (1930). He dealt with Tepoztlán, a Mexican village which had, according to the 1921 Mexican census, a population of 3,836 (Redfield 1930: 170). Another approach, the study of the urban background of the Mexican immigrant, still remains to be investigated. As Ruth Tuck (1946: 77–8) has pointed out in her study of a Mexican-American minority group:

It is too bad that the typical small *mestizo* town, with its satellite *ranchos* and *pueblos*, has not been the object of study by some sociologist or anthropologist. Many primitive Mexican groups have been so examined, as well as one or two folk groups where Aztec custom had strong survival. But life in Sombrerete, Zacatecas, or Celaya, Guanajuato, or Los Reyes, Michoacan, can be reconstructed only from casual observation or from the stories of its former residents. A scientific examination of them, today, might still aid in understanding the background of our Mexican immigrants. The events of the Mexican Revolution and the subsequent educational and agrarian reforms have

made changes, it is true, but it is not improbable that a large stock of custom and tradition survives only slightly changed. I have been impressed with the fact that accounts of daily life in these districts, given by agricultural workers recently imported from there, tally in many aspects with the reminiscences of the immigrant who left twenty-five years ago.

The method used by Redfield in his Tepoztlán study was that of an ethnographer. This method is well suited to the study of people in a small and relatively homogeneous rural community. For a study of a particular group of people in an urban community, however, the writer's method of studying language usage might be advantageously employed, since we are not so much interested in the complex social organization, per se, as in the cultural equipment of the potential immigrant.

A further advantage of this linguistic method lies in the fact that it provides a means of ascertaining the relative importance of folk and urban influences in the cultural background of the individual. In part, these influences would be revealed in the daily conversation of the individual. As this material accumulated, it could be supplemented by interviews and questionnaires of the type used in the Tucson study.

The Study of Mexican-American Bilinguals

The present study has been concerned largely with the special question of how language functions among Mexican-American bilingual individuals within a single American community. This investigation has left untouched many related problems — some more inclusive and some less inclusive in scope. Several of these problems, all dealing specifically with the Mexican-American bilingual minority group, will now be outlined and an approach to the study of each suggested.

Language Usage and Personality Structure

An important question asked but left unanswered in this study concerns the relation of changes in the language usage of bilingual Mexicans to changes in personality structure. Does language function differently in the lives of individuals having different types of personality? This is one of many questions on the psychological level of investigation, and should be studied with the aid of psychological techniques. Some of the relations between language and personality have been outlined by Sapir (1927); and Newman (1941) has made a detailed case study of the language adjustment of an adolescent high-school boy. Newman checked his linguistic analysis of the boy's personality with a psychiatrist's psychological analysis of the same individual, and found a high degree of correlation. The next step along this line would seem to be the linguistic and psychological analysis of a whole series of such cases in a single social setting. The problem would then be to describe and classify the various psychological types, with the aid of the Rorschach, thematic apperception, and other such tests not dependent on linguistic skill, and to see whether there are linguistic types corresponding to the psychological types. For an investigator with anthropological training, a bilingual community would be a good place to make such a study, since, as we have seen, the bilingual's use of alternate languages to define interpersonal relations greatly facilitates observation and analysis of language usage. The outcome of such a study might be expected to show to what extent language usage could be used to supplement existing personality tests, and also whether it could be used as an alternative to such tests.

Language Usage as Life History Data

The study of life histories has come to be regarded as a highly specialized and valuable method of sociological analysis. This method already has proved of much value in studying the process of acculturation. Yet, as far as is known to the writer, relatively little attention has been paid to the successive changes in linguistic behavior, in relation to different stages in the life history. How is it that some individuals who turned away from their ancestral culture and language in youth may in later life develop a strong sentimental attachment to them, while other individuals, perhaps even in the same family, may continue to deny any affiliation? The study of how language functions in successive periods of a bilingual individual's life would seem to offer a new approach to the individual's value system and to the events in his life which are of greatest sociological significance. There are two methods of obtaining such material. One is through depth interviews in which the individual is encouraged to tell anecdotal material about his reaction to and use of language. The other is through periodic field observations at one- or two-year intervals on the actual language usage of the

individual in standardized situations. It should be emphasized that both methods are dependent upon a thorough knowledge of the sociological and linguistic background of the community in which the life history's subjects live.

Language Usage of Subgroups

In the course of this study, we have noted that language seems to be intimately connected with the functioning of various subgroups in the ethnic community. Among these are the family, the neighborhood gang, the group of preschool-age children, various occupational groups, and social cliques. Much remains to be learned about the relation of these various subgroups to the acculturation process. Do they speed the process, retard it, or leave it unaffected? What attitudes, values, do they tend to develop within their members? Some suggestions may now be made as to how language usage may be employed to answer these questions.

Preschool-age Children — This study has referred briefly to linguistic and other social behavior of preschool-age children of Mexican descent. From the data obtained, it appears that these children are largely monolingual before entering school. The beginning of school, then, marks the beginning of bilinguality for many children. How does the sudden switch from Spanish to English during school hours affect the child's attitudes and values? Has the introduction (in 1946) of weekly Spanish lessons in all Tucson public schools made any change in the situation? To answer these questions it would be useful to examine the linguistic and social behavior of a large number of five- and six-year-old children during the period immediately before and following their enrollment in school. The results might be expected to show how the child's school experience affects his conception of his relation to the ethnic and general community.

The procedure in the inquiry would include the periodic sampling of the linguistic behavior of these preschool and first-year schoolchildren in all of their social relations. In addition to linguistic behavior in standardized situations, these samples would include examples of the child's English and Spanish vocabularies, verbal responses to pictures, and also his stock of nursery rhymes, folklore, superstitions, and so forth, in both English and Spanish. For comparative purposes, samples would be taken of the linguistic behavior of children in different types of families and in different neighborhoods. The end results might be expected to indicate how the process of becoming bilingual affects the assimilation of these children into the general community.

Adolescent Bilingual Children — In this study we have seen how the condition of being midway between cultures leaves many teen-age children feeling that they are neither Mexican nor American. We also have seen how, in situations in which family members can not achieve desired goals, the teen-age children may revolt and seek to form a society of their own. The social process leading to the formation of the Pachuco-type gang, together with the language usage of gang members inside and outside their families, could well form the subject of a separate study.

Such a study might begin with a detailed investigation of the home life of the various members of one Pachuco gang. The origin and social organization of the gang could then be studied against the background of family structure and neighborhood. This would lead up to a detailed study of the language usage and social participation of various gang members inside and outside the gang. Some of the questions which this investigation might be expected to answer are: What does the gang's vocabulary reveal as to the attitudes and interests of the members? To what extent may the individual's use of Pachuco and pochismo words be taken as an index of his marginality in the social system of the community? Judging from verbal symbolization, what are the main sources of the standards of evaluation on which the goals of gang members are based? How, if at all, is the influence, positive or negative, of church, school, and other institutions reflected in the linguistically defined categories of interpersonal relations?

Families of Mixed Marriages — Reference has been made in this thesis to some instances of intermarriage between Mexicans and Americans in Tucson (see Chapter 8). In cases in which the couple takes up residence in the barrio, the tendency seems to be for Spanish to be the language of the family, regardless of the Anglo background of one parent. It would be interesting to study a number of such families in different parts of a town such as Tucson, and to see what language usage reveals as to the interpersonal relations of the members of the various Anglo-Mexican and Mexican-Anglo families in the Tucson social system. An opportunity also would be offered for evaluation of the comparative social pressure exerted by Anglo versus Mexican family structure, through examining the language use between parents, children, and relatives on both sides of the family.

On a more inclusive level, it would be useful to obtain precise figures on the intermarriage rate between Anglos and Mexicans within the class system. This could be followed up by an analysis of any changes in ethnic status and language usage accompanying intermarriage in various classes. Are the mixed families in each class usually assimilated into the Anglo community? Do they tend to form a separate group of their own? Or are they usually relegated to the Mexican community? What changes in the language usage and interpersonal relations of various family members may be expected to accompany each of these three types of social adjustment?

Cliques — In the study of social mobility, cliques are a highly important subject since they constitute one of the chief mechanisms through which an individual achieves higher social status. For the bilingual individual seeking to move in Anglo social circles, they present a serious problem, since neither his informal Spanish-English mixture nor his formal English would seem adequate for the sophisticated Anglo-type group. How then do bilinguals solve this problem? Are there "intermediate cliques" in which some Hispanicization is permissible? Can the individual learn upper-class Anglo "bon mots" inside such a clique or must he go to other sources? The study of the language usage of a connected series of cliques, some inside and some outside the ethnic community, might be expected to throw new light on the process of bilingual assimilation.

Occupational Groups — Our sociological survey of Tucson has indicated that the bulk of the Mexican population is occupationally subordinate to the Anglo group. Mexicans and Indians are the mainstay of the town's labor supply. As a partial consequence of this, there are many occupational groups composed largely of Mexican skilled and unskilled laborers. Outstanding examples of this may be found in the building industry, in city and county road crews, in agricultural labor, mining, in the Southern Pacific shops, and in ranching (Seibold

1946). The language usage within such groups could advantageously be studied both from the standpoint of interpersonal relations within the group and from that of interpersonal relations between members and Anglo employers. Do Mexican employees of different statuses differ in their ways of speaking to their supervisors? Does the supervisor have to show a command of the type of Spanish current among the laboring group to gain the confidence of his men? The answers to such questions might be expected to reveal new evidence on how the occupational structure in the community affects the processes of acculturation and assimilation.

Other Bilingual Communities

In the present study the problem has centered entirely in a Mexican-American community in which the bilinguals studied occupied a subordinate position in the town's social structure. They did have some representation in all but the topmost social class, and in this respect they differed sharply from the town's Negro population. For the purposes of comparison, it now would be useful to examine by means of language usage the interpersonal relations and attitudes of bilinguals in two other contrasting social systems; one, a community in which the bilinguals move freely in the topmost social circles on a basis of full equality with the top Anglos, and, the other, one in which the bilinguals were entirely at the bottom of the social ladder. A social system of the first type might be found in a border town such as Nogales, Arizona, in which American public officials have married into Mexican families of high social prestige. A social system of the second type might be found in an interior town such as Redlands, California, where

the Mexican population traditionally has consisted solely of agricultural laborers and their families. In those two communities the position of bilingual individuals probably would be found to differ radically in their relation to the field of interpersonal relations operating in each community. Thus, the comparison would seem to provide a further test of the propositions advanced in the Tucson study.

Bilingual Areas and Political Borders

Finally, a note may be added on the need for extending this type of research to other frontier areas. The sociological problems arising from the drawing of boundary lines through a zone in which two cultures mingle are not confined to southern Arizona. We may predict that similar problems will exist wherever international boundaries are established between contiguous cultures having different languages. We also may predict that in any such area there will be a large number of bilinguals, and that these will tend to develop a hybrid culture and language of their own. "Assimilation" in such an environment thus takes on a significance quite different from the traditional ethnocentric use of the term. In the long run, the assimilation process in such areas would seem to consist not so much in the engulfing of a minority group by a majority group as the fusion of the two to produce something new. If such is found to be the case, a modification of traditional political and educational policies with respect to such border peoples would seem in order. Perhaps statesmanship based on the recognition of the fact that borders are not lines but distinct cultural zones would provide a basis for a reduction of friction along the world's numerous political frontiers.

REFERENCES

ARMBRUSTER, GORDON H.
  1944   An Analysis of Ideologies in the Context of Discussion. *The American Journal of Sociology,* Vol. L, No. 2, pp. 123–33. University of Chicago Press, Chicago.

BARKER, GEORGE C.
  1943   *Functions of the Ancestral Language Among American Immigrants.* MS, master's thesis, University of Chicago, Chicago.
  1950   Pachuco: An American-Spanish Argot and Its Social Functions in Tucson, Arizona. *Social Science Bulletin,* No. 18, University of Arizona Press, Tucson.

BLOCH, BERNARD AND GEORGE L. TRAGER
  1942   *Outline of Linguistic Analysis.* Linguistic Society of America, Baltimore.

BLOOMFIELD, LEONARD
  1933   *Language.* Henry Holt and Company, New York.

BOSSARD, JAMES H. S.
  1945   The Bilingual as a Person — Linguistic Identification with Status. *American Sociological Review,* Vol. X, No. 6, pp. 699–709. American Sociological Society, Menasha.

BROWN, J. F.
  1936   *Psychology and the Social Order.* McGraw-Hill, New York.

CHASE, STUART
  1939   *The Tyranny of Words.* Harcourt, Brace and Company, New York.

CHILD, IRVIN L.
  1943   *Italian or American? The Second Generation in Conflict.* Yale University Press, New Haven.

CUERVO, RUFINO J.
  1935   *El castellano en América.* Biblioteca Aldeana de Colombia, Bogotá.

DE LAGUNA, GRACE A.
  1927   *Speech: Its Function and Development.* Yale University Press, New Haven.

DEWEY, JOHN
  1925   *Experience and Nature.* Open Court Publishing Company, Chicago and London.

DOROZEWSKI, W.
  1933   Quelques remarques sur les rapports de la sociologie et de la linguistique: Durkheim et F. de Saussure. *Psychologie du Langage.* Paris.

ENTWISTLE, WILLIAM J.
  1936   *The Spanish Language.* Faber and Faber, London.

GETTY, HARRY T.
  1943–46 Unpublished Interview Notes. On file Arizona State Museum Library, University of Arizona, Tucson.

GOODMAN, JOHN K.

1942   *Race and Race Mixture as the Basis of Social Status in Tucson, Arizona.* MS, bachelor of arts thesis, Yale University, New Haven.

HAYAKAWA, S. I.

1941   *Language in Action.* Harcourt, Brace and Company, New York.

HENRIQUEZ URENA, PEDRO

1938   *Sobre el Problema del andalucismo dialectal de América.* Madrid (for University of Buenos Aires, Buenos Aires).

HUMPHREY, NORMAN D.

1944   The Changing Structure of the Detroit Mexican Family. *American Sociological Review,* Vol. 9, No. 6, pp. 622–26. American Sociological Society, Menasha.

JOHNSON, JEAN BASSETT

1943   A Clear Case of Linguistic Acculturation. *American Anthropologist,* Vol. XLV, No. 3, pp. 427–35. Menasha.

KARDINER, ABRAM

1945   *The Psychological Frontiers of Society.* Columbia University Press, New York.

KORZYBSKI, ALFRED

1933   *Science and Sanity.* Science Press, Lancaster.

LEE, I. J.

1941   *Language Habits and Human Affairs.* Harper and Brothers, New York.

LORIMER, FRANK

1929   *The Growth of Reason.* Harcourt, Brace and Company, New York.

MALINOWSKI, BRONISLAW

1923   Supplement to *The Meaning of Meaning.* Charles C. K. Ogden and I. A. Richards. K. Paul, Trench, Trubner and Company, Ltd. London.

MANNHEIM, KARL

1936   *Ideology and Utopia.* Harcourt, Brace and Company, New York.

McGRANAHAN, DONALD V.

1936   The Psychology of Language. *Psychological Bulletin,* Vol. 33, No. 3, pp. 179–216. American Psychological Association, Princeton.

MEAD, GEORGE H.

1931   Thought, Symbols and Language. Reprinted in *Source Book for Social Psychology,* edited by Kimball Young. F. S. Crofts and Company, New York.

1934   *Mind, Seif and Society.* University of Chicago Press, Chicago.

MILLER, NEAL E. AND JOHN DOLLARD

1941   *Social Learning and Imitation.* Yale University Press, New Haven.

MORRIS, CHARLES W.

1938   Foundations of the Theory of Signs, *International Encyclopedia of Unified Science,* Vol. I, No. 2. University of Chicago Press, Chicago.

NEWMAN, STANLEY S.

1941   Behavior Patterns in Linguistic Structure: A Case Study. In *Language, Culture and Personality,* Leslie Spier, A. Irving Hallowell, and Stanley S. Newman, eds. Sapir Memorial Publication Fund. Menasha.

PIAGET, JEAN

1926   *The Language and Thought of the Child.* Harcourt, Brace and Company, New York.

POST, ANITA C.

1934   Southern Arizona Spanish Phonology. *Humanities Bulletin,* No. 1, University of Arizona, Tucson.

REDFIELD, ROBERT

1930   *Tepoztlan: A Mexican Village.* University of Chicago Press, Chicago.

REUTER, EDWARD BYRON

1946   Culture Contacts in Puerto Rico. *The American Journal of Sociology,* Vol. LII, No. 2, pp. 91–101. University of Chicago Press, Chicago.

ROGLER, CHARLES C.

1944   The Role of Semantics in the Study of Race Distance in Puerto Rico. *Social Forces,* Vol. 22, No. 4, pp. 448–53. University of North Carolina Press, Chapel Hill.

SAPIR, EDWARD

1927   Speech as a Personality Trait. *The American Journal of Sociology,* Vol. XXXII, No. 6. University of Chicago Press, Chicago.

1933   Language. *Encyclopedia of the Social Sciences,* Vol. IX, pp. 155–68. The Macmillan Company, New York.

SCHLAUCH, MARGARET

1942   *The Gift of Tongues.* Modern Age Book, New York.

SEIBOLD, DORIS K.

1946   *Localisms in the Spoken English of the Cattle Industry of Santa Cruz County, Arizona.* MS, master's thesis, University of Arizona, Tucson.

SOBARZO, HORACIO

1955   *Crónica de la Aventura de Raousset-Boulbon.* Librería de Manuel Porrúa, S. A., Mexico, D.F.

SPICER, EDWARD H.

1943   Linguistic Aspects of Yaqui Acculturation. *American Anthropologist,* Vol. XLV, No. 3, pp. 410–27. Menasha.

TRAGER, GEORGE L.

1941   *Number, Gender, and Personal Reference in Pennsylvania Windish (Slovene).* Unpublished paper read before the Linguistic Society of America. Baltimore.

TUCK, RUTH D.

1946   *Not with the Fist: A Study of Mexican-Americans in a Southwest City.* Harcourt, Brace and Company, New York.

VENDRYES, JOSEPH

 1925   *Language: A Linguistic Introduction to History*. A. A. Knopf, New York.

WARNER, W. LLOYD AND PAUL S. LUNT

 1941   *The Social Life of a Modern Community*. Yale University Press, New Haven.

WHITE, LESLIE A.

 1940   The Symbol: The Origin and Basis of Human Behavior. *Philosophy of Science,* Vol. 7, October. Baltimore.